Italian Light and Easy

Italian Light and Easy

More than 100 Delicious and Healthy Recipes Lower in Fat and Calories

Pasquale Bruno, Jr.

To Arlene
Con Amore
Pasquale Bruno

CB
CONTEMPORARY
BOOKS
CHICAGO

Library of Congress Cataloging-in-Publication Data

Bruno, Pasquale.
    Italian light and easy : more than 100 delicious and healthy recipes
lower in fat and calories / Pasquale Bruno, Jr.
        p.   cm.
    Includes index.
    ISBN 0-8092-3858-6 (pbk.)
    1. Cookery, Italian.   2. Low-fat diet—Recipes.   3. Low-calorie
diet—Recipes.   I. Title.
TX723.B744   1993
641.5945—dc20

        92-46326
        CIP

Other Books by Pasquale Bruno, Jr.
The Great Chicago-Style Pizza Cookbook
Pasta Tecnica

On front cover: *Cioppino* (Fish Stew), see page 98

Published by Contemporary Books, Inc.
180 North Michigan Avenue, Chicago, Illinois 60601
Manufactured in the United States of America
International Standard Book Number: 0-8092-3858-6

Contents

Italian
Light
and
Easy

This collection of recipes grew for the most part out of the classes that I teach at my cooking school, Cucina Paradiso, in Chicago. There was one series of classes in particular, however, that thrust the idea of this book forward. Those classes were called "Italian, Light and Easy." The idea behind the series was to put together recipes that had a total preparation and cooking time of less than an hour. Additionally my goal was to make the recipes low in fat, cholesterol, and calories—without sacrificing one iota of flavor.

As the recipes and ideas started to flow it became apparent that my goal of creating healthy *and* flavorful food would be easier to reach than I had at first thought, and it didn't take me too long to figure out why; for the most part my style of Italian cooking had always been light and easy. My southern Italian roots had always grown in that direction. For example: using olive oil instead of butter and cream; grilling or sautéing instead of deep-frying; an abundant use of vegetables (all of them from the garden behind our house) with pasta, as a salad or a side dish; the seafood and nonmeat dishes that my mother creatively came up with during the long Lenten periods each year; and the various succession of soups throughout the winter months, most of them with beans, pasta, or both.

Those fragrant and aromatic fresh herbs from the garden played a major role in intensifying the flavor of any dish. And it was rare to have a red sauce for pasta that was not made from the tomatoes that my mother canned each year—more than 200 quarts, each with two or three leaves of fresh basil. Though I certainly didn't think about it at the time, I was eating Italian food that was in fact light and healthy.

I guess the tomato doesn't fall far from the vine. The methods and ideas that my mother (and my aunts and uncles, too) used in the preparation and cooking of Italian dishes not only stayed with me but also have become even more ingrained over the past 10 years. So as the recipes for this book started to take shape, I was ever mindful of my goals—light and easy—but some break with tradition was unavoidable.

For example, my mother made frittate using whole eggs, egg substitutes not being available at that time. I wanted a frittata chapter in this book for a few reasons: it is not only an easy dish to make and delicious, too, but it also is very versatile, as it can be served for brunch, breakfast, or at a late-night meal. My first attempt at using an egg substitute (I actually tried several brands and found them all to be of equal quality) in a frittata was a rousing success. It had all the goodness I could ask for without the guilt.

In the soup chapter, the Escarole and Potato Soup with Beans underwent minor culinary surgery. Traditionally this soup is made with Italian sausage, beans, and escarole. I eliminated the Italian sausage and added potatoes. The goodness and flavor is still there, but much of the fat is gone. And I continued to think that way. Keep the flavor and goodness of each dish intact but reduce the fat, the cholesterol, and as many calories as possible. In most of the recipes I've allowed for a range of servings with the lower number being a more generous portion. Calorie counts have been calculated based on the higher number of servings, however, and optional ingredients and recipe variations have not been included in the calorie determinations.

The "easy" part of the recipes, though obviously intertwined with the "light," posed a similar set of circumstances. In this regard I did not always connect "easy" with speed. Though most of the recipes can be done rather quickly—preparation and cooking time in less than an hour—there are cases where time, by necessity, is extended. Making dough for pizza and focaccia, for example. Obviously the time it takes for the dough to rise is longer than an hour, but the total work time—mixing and kneading—is still relatively short. Making your own stocks for soups is another example. While it may take several hours to properly intensify the flavor of a stock, the actual work time to prepare and combine the ingredients is quite short.

Also, I have linked "easy" with convenience. A number of recipes can be used in different ways. Caponata, for example, can be used as an antipasto, a side dish, or even spread over a slice of grilled Italian bread for a tasty snack. Several of the pasta and vegetable dishes—Noodles with Oil, Garlic, and Escarole and Ziti with Broccoli and Chick-Peas—can be served at room temperature as well as hot. Focaccia can be sliced and grilled for bruschetta or crostini. A batch of dough for gnocchi can be cut in half and frozen for convenient use another time.

Be my guest and enjoy with me Italian dishes that are rich with the flavors of Italy and truly light and easy.

Mangia bene!

Pasquale Bruno, Jr.

There was an uncle in our family whom we called "Mr. Soup." From the first day of cold weather on through spring he would make soup—every day he made soup. He never made an uninteresting zuppa; his soups were thick with ingredients and jumping with flavor. Sometimes you couldn't find the broth for the vegetables and pasta, and sometimes the soup was so thick you could stand a spoon in it, but never did he make a soup that wasn't a bowl-scraping delight.

I guess I share his ideas of what a soup should be—thick and hearty and full of intense flavors. My uncle would say, "There is nothing worse than a weak soup." If he were still around, I think he would enjoy my soup collection, because there's not a weak one in the bunch. When all the students in one of my soup classes came back for seconds on Escarole and Potato Soup with Beans, I knew it was a winner. And the way my students raved about the Roasted Eggplant and Sun-Dried Tomato Soup put a smile on my face.

The Pasta and Bean Soup is a classic, a favorite of mine for as long as I can remember my mother making it (at least once a week). As I think about it now, I know why she used her biggest pot for this soup—my brothers and I did some very serious spoon work on this delicious "pasta fazool," to the accompaniment of a couple of loaves of Italian bread.

It seems to me that I really had my uncle in mind when I put together the recipe for Everything Soup, which is packed with a variety of vegetables, beans, and lentils.

A well-made soup will warm both body and soul, and I guess that's why my uncle relied on them when there was a chill in the air. But soups have another benefit as well: substantial and filling, they're perfect entrees for lunch and dinner. And, in fact, some experts have suggested that the warming quality of a bowl of soup served as a first course suppresses one's appetite for the meal that follows.

When convenience has led me to substitute canned chicken broth for homemade stock, I use the lower-salt type. Should you wish to defat the broth, put it in a bowl and refrigerate overnight. The next day, skim the fat off the surface.

Brodo di Pollo

(Chicken Stock)

....

1. Place the chicken pieces in a large stockpot. Add the cold water and bring to a boil, skimming off scum that comes to the surface. Reduce the heat to a simmer and add the remaining ingredients. Simmer the stock, uncovered, for 2 hours, skimming as necessary. Add hot water as needed to keep the same level of liquid in the pot.

2. Remove the chicken parts from the stock. Strain the stock through two layers of dampened cheesecloth or a fine-mesh strainer. Cool, then refrigerate overnight.

3. The next day, skim off the fat that has collected on top. Keep the stock refrigerated for up to 5 or 6 days or freeze it in small containers or an ice cube tray. If refrigerated, bring the stock to a boil after 3 days, let it cool, and return it to the refrigerator.

2 pounds chicken pieces (wings, legs, thighs, backs)
4 quarts cold water
2 ribs celery (with leaves), cut into 1-inch pieces
2 large carrots, scraped and cut into 1-inch pieces
1 medium-size yellow onion, peeled and cut in half
5–6 sprigs fresh parsley
1 bay leaf
8 black peppercorns
2 cloves
1 teaspoon salt

Makes about 3 quarts
Calories: 40 per 1-cup serving

Brodo Bianco di Vitello

(White Veal Stock)

This stock can be used in place of others in any of the following soup recipes.

....

2 pounds meaty veal knuckles
10 cups cold water
1 large yellow onion, peeled
  and cut in half
2 small leeks, cleaned and cut
  in half
1 carrot, scraped and cut into
  1-inch pieces
2 ribs celery, cut into 1-inch
  pieces
1 teaspoon salt
1 bouquet garni: 6 parsley
  sprigs, ¼ teaspoon dried
  thyme, and 1 bay leaf in a
  cheesecloth bag
1 pound chicken backs and
  thighs, skin removed

1. In a large stockpot, cover the veal bones with the cold water. Bring to a boil, skimming off the fat.

2. Add the onion, leeks, carrot, celery, salt, and bouquet garni. Lower the heat and simmer, uncovered, for 2 hours. In the last hour of cooking, add the chicken. Skim off any fat that rises to the surface.

3. Strain the stock through a double layer of dampened cheesecloth or a fine-mesh strainer. Cool, then refrigerate overnight. The next day, carefully skim the fat off the surface. Keep the stock refrigerated for up to 5 or 6 days or freeze it in small containers or an ice cube tray. If refrigerated, bring the stock to a boil after 3 days, let it cool, and return it to the refrigerator.

Makes about 6 cups
Calories: 40 per 1-cup serving

Brodo Scuro di Carne

(Brown Stock)

This stock can be used in place of others in any of the following soup recipes.

....

1. Place the bones in a large stockpot with the water. Bring to a boil, skimming scum off the surface as it appears. Reduce the heat and simmer, uncovered, for 30 minutes.

2. Add the remaining ingredients to the pot. Bring to a boil. Reduce the heat and simmer, uncovered, for 2 hours. Strain the stock through two layers of dampened cheesecloth or a fine-mesh strainer. Cool the stock for about an hour, then refrigerate overnight. The next day, skim any fat off the top. Keep the stock refrigerated for up to 5 or 6 days or freeze it in small containers or an ice cube tray. If refrigerated, bring the stock to a boil after 3 days, let it cool, and return it to the refrigerator.

6 pounds lean beef shin bones
5 quarts cold water
1 large carrot, scraped and diced
2 ribs celery, diced
1 medium-size yellow onion, diced
1 cup drained canned plum tomatoes
1 bouquet garni: 8–10 black peppercorns, 4 cloves, 1 bay leaf, 1 teaspoon dried thyme, a few sprigs fresh parsley in a cheesecloth bag

Makes 2½ to 3 quarts
Calories: 24 per 1-cup serving

Zuppa di Patate, Scarola, e Fagioli

(Escarole and Potato Soup with Beans)

When I created this recipe some 20 years ago, I used savoy cabbage, but I have found that escarole adds a softer texture and a cleaner flavor. Escarole should be considered in cooked dishes as well as salad. Its sharp flavor adds another dimension of taste to soups, and it can be sautéed and served as a side dish or tossed with pasta. This soup cries out for garlic, so if your garlic cloves are running on the small side you might wish to add one or two additional.

....

½ cup chopped yellow onion
1½ pounds (about 12 small) red-skinned potatoes, cubed
2 tablespoons virgin olive oil
4 cloves garlic, chopped fine
6 cups Chicken Stock (see Index) or lower-salt canned chicken broth
1 cup water
2 tablespoons chopped flat-leaf parsley
1 15-ounce can cannellini beans, drained and rinsed
1 pound escarole, cleaned and coarsely chopped
salt and freshly ground black pepper to taste
4–6 tablespoons freshly grated Parmesan cheese

1. In a large pot over medium-low heat, sauté the onion and potatoes in the olive oil until the onion just starts to soften, 2 to 3 minutes. Add the garlic and cook and stir for 2 minutes.

2. Add the chicken stock, water, and parsley. Bring the soup to a boil, reduce the heat, and simmer, uncovered, for 25 to 30 minutes or until the potatoes are just tender.

3. Add the beans and the escarole and simmer gently until the escarole wilts—about 5 minutes. Add the salt and pepper.

4. Top each serving of soup with a tablespoon of grated Parmesan cheese or pass separately.

_____

Serves 4 to 6
Calories: 258 per serving

Pasta e Fagioli

(Pasta and Bean Soup)

Pasta and bean soup is one of the treasures of Venetian cooking. To cut out a lot of the fat, I have eliminated the pancetta or salt pork that is sometimes sautéed in the oil at the beginning. Nonetheless, this version is hearty and flavorful. A simple green salad and some crusty Italian bread are all that is needed for a complete and nutritious meal.

1. In a heavy 4- to 5-quart pot over low heat, sauté the onion in the olive oil until soft and translucent, 2 to 3 minutes. Add the garlic and cook and stir for 1 minute. Add the stock, bay leaf, water, tomatoes, and tomato puree. Cook at a bare simmer, uncovered, stirring occasionally, for 45 minutes. Add the salt and pepper.

2. About 10 minutes before you are ready to serve the soup, cook the pasta in 4 quarts of boiling salted water until al dente (do not overcook). When you start cooking the pasta, add the beans to the soup and heat thoroughly. In some parts of Italy a portion of the beans (about one-quarter the total amount) is passed through a food mill into the pot to thicken the consistency.

3. Drain the pasta and divide it among serving bowls. Ladle the beans and broth over the pasta.

4. Serve the grated Parmesan cheese and red pepper flakes on the side.

½ cup chopped yellow onion
¼ cup virgin olive oil
2 cloves garlic, crushed
1¾ cups Brown Stock (see Index) or 1 13¾-ounce can lower-salt beef broth
1 bay leaf
1 quart water
1 28-ounce can plum tomatoes, with juice, crushed by hand in the can
1 16-ounce can tomato puree
Salt and freshly ground black pepper to taste
½ pound tubetti or ditalini pasta
1 19-ounce can cannellini beans, drained and rinsed
Freshly grated Parmesan cheese for serving
Crushed red pepper flakes for serving

Serves 6 to 8
Calories: 266 per serving

Tutto Zuppa

(Everything Soup)

Everything Soup is simply my version of a lusty vegetable soup with lentils added for extra nutrition and flavor. Once the ingredients have been made ready for the pot, the whole process—from start to soup on the table—takes only 35 minutes.

....

½ pound dried lentils
2 tablespoons virgin olive oil
½ cup chopped yellow onion
½ cup chopped red bell
　　pepper
1 clove garlic, minced
1 cup chopped zucchini
½ cup (about ¼ pound)
　　sliced fresh mushrooms
½ cup chopped trimmed fresh
　　fennel bulb
1 28-ounce can plum
　　tomatoes, with juice
1 quart Chicken Stock (see
　　Index) or lower-salt canned
　　chicken broth
1 19-ounce can cannellini or
　　Great Northern beans,
　　drained and rinsed
Salt and freshly ground black
　　pepper to taste

1. In a saucepan over medium-high heat, cook the lentils in simmering water to cover until they are barely tender—about 10 minutes. Drain and reserve.

2. In a large pot over medium heat, heat the oil. Add the onion, bell pepper, and garlic and sauté for 3 minutes. Add the zucchini, mushrooms, and fennel and stir and cook for 2 minutes more.

3. Add the juice from the can of tomatoes to the pot. Crush the tomatoes in the can with your hand and add them to the pot. Add the chicken stock or broth.

4. Bring the soup to an easy boil, then reduce the heat to maintain a steady simmer. Simmer, uncovered, for 20 minutes. Add the lentils and simmer for 10 minutes more. Add the beans and simmer for 5 minutes more. Add the salt and pepper and serve the soup hot.

_____

Serves 4 to 6
Calories: 302 per serving

Zuppa Bandiera

(Pasta and Chick-Pea Soup with Sun-Dried Tomatoes)

I have named this recipe *Zuppa Bandiera*, or "flag soup," for the colors of the main ingredients, which in turn are the colors of the Italian flag. The soup has a variety of textures, and the pronounced flavor of the sun-dried tomatoes is most appealing. Serve the soup as a main dish with crusty Italian bread or bruschetta (see Index).

....

1. In a large pot over medium heat, warm the olive oil for 1 minute. Add the onion and garlic and sauté for 2 minutes. Add the stock, water, parsley, chick-peas, celery, and rosemary.

2. Raise the heat to medium-high and bring the soup to a boil. Reduce the heat and simmer, uncovered, stirring occasionally, for 30 minutes.

3. Add the sun-dried tomatoes and pasta. Simmer, partially covered, until the pasta is al dente. Thin the soup with water if necessary. Add the salt and pepper. Pass the Parmesan cheese separately.

Serves 4 to 6
Calories: 208 per serving

2 tablespoons virgin olive oil
½ cup chopped yellow onion
2 cloves garlic, minced
1 quart Chicken Stock (see Index) or lower-salt canned chicken broth
1 cup water
¼ cup minced flat-leaf parsley
1 15-ounce can chick-peas, drained and rinsed
½ cup chopped celery
½ teaspoon dried rosemary, crumbled
½ cup drained oil-packed sun-dried tomatoes, patted dry and chopped
3 ounces (about 1 cup) short spinach pasta (farfalle, gnocchi, elbow)
Salt and freshly ground black pepper to taste
Freshly grated Parmesan cheese for serving (optional)

Zuppa di Pomodoro e Basilico con Crostone

(Tomato and Basil Soup with Garlic Bruschetta)

An excellent summer luncheon soup that requires only a simple green salad to round out the meal. Do not substitute dried basil for fresh; the tomatoes need the fragrance of fresh basil. But the ingredient that really makes this soup wonderful is the garlic-rubbed slice of bread that goes on top.

....

2 tablespoons extra-virgin olive oil

2 large cloves garlic, peeled and sliced in half

2 28-ounce cans plum tomatoes, drained

2 cups Chicken Stock (see Index) or lower-salt canned chicken broth

16 fresh basil leaves, washed and torn in half

Salt and freshly ground black pepper to taste

4 ½-inch-thick slices Italian bread

2 cloves garlic, peeled

4 teaspoons freshly grated Parmesan cheese

1. In a large pot over medium heat, warm the olive oil for 1 minute. Add the halved garlic cloves and cook and stir until the cloves turn a light brown (do not burn). Discard the garlic.

2. Crush the tomatoes in the can with your hand and add to the pot. Add the stock and basil. Bring the soup to a gentle boil, reduce the heat, and maintain a steady simmer, uncovered, until the soup thickens (about 20 minutes). Add the salt and pepper.

3. While the soup is reducing, toast the bread on both sides under a preheated broiler. Remove the toast from the oven and, while still hot, rub one side of the toast briskly with the peeled garlic. Set aside.

4. Ladle the hot soup into bowls. Place one piece of toast on top of the soup in each bowl. Top each piece of toast with 1 teaspoon freshly grated Parmesan cheese. Serve at once.

Serves 4
Calories: 228 per serving

Bruschetta and Crostini

Bruschetta: The classic preparation is this: Toast or grill slices of Italian bread. While the bread is still warm, rub the surface of the bread with a peeled clove of garlic and then dress it with extra-virgin olive oil and some freshly ground pepper. Properly speaking, this is called *fettunta*, or bread with olive oil. A more Americanized version of bruschetta is the addition of chopped fresh tomatoes and torn leaves of fresh basil. More elaborate versions of bruschetta include the addition of chopped olives, capers, even a dusting of grated Parmesan cheese.

Crostini: Crostini is similar to a canape. After rounds (or squares or diamond shapes) of bread are toasted, they are spread or garnished with, for example, anchovies, cheese, seafood, flavored butters, and various types of meats.

Zuppa di Melanzane Arrostite con Pomodori Secchi

(Roasted Eggplant and Sun-Dried Tomato Soup)

Roasting the eggplant instead of sautéing it drastically reduces the amount of oil required, but just as important, the roasting gives the eggplant a smoky flavor. A definite plus to this soup is that it can be served hot or cold, so it becomes a soup for all seasons. Serve with crusty Italian bread or garlic bruschetta (see preceding recipe).

....

2 pounds firm eggplant, peeled and cut into 1-inch cubes
¼ cup virgin olive oil
4 grinds of black pepper
½ cup chopped yellow onion
½ cup drained oil-packed sun-dried tomatoes, patted dry
2 cloves garlic, put through a press
¼ cup chopped flat-leaf parsley
3¼ cups Chicken Stock (see Index) or 2 13-ounce cans lower-salt canned chicken broth
1⅔ cups (1 13-ounce can) water
¼ teaspoon dried thyme, crumbled
Freshly grated Parmesan cheese for serving

1. Preheat the oven to 375°F. Place the eggplant in a large shallow baking pan or sheet pan in a single layer. Drizzle 2 tablespoons of the olive oil over the eggplant. Grind the pepper evenly over the eggplant. Roast the eggplant for about 25 minutes, turning it twice, until tender.

2. Meanwhile, add the remaining olive oil to a skillet set over medium heat. Sauté the onion, sun-dried tomatoes, garlic, and parsley for 2 to 3 minutes, until the onion softens. Set aside.

3. Put the stock, water, and thyme in a 3- to 4-quart pot. Bring to a boil, then reduce the heat to maintain a steady simmer.

4. Place the roasted eggplant and onion/sun-dried tomato mixture in a food processor fitted with the steel blade. Process until a smooth puree is formed.

5. Add the puree to the stock and stir well. Heat through, but do not boil. Let cool slightly before serving or refrigerate and serve chilled. Pass the Parmesan cheese separately.

Serves 4 to 6
Calories: 172 per serving

I never let a day pass without having a salad. It might be a simple salad of romaine or leaf lettuce with tomato or red onion, or it might be something a bit more exotic like a panzanella salad or Bean and Tuna Salad with Radicchio.

The one kind I will not tolerate is a boring salad—those made with hard lettuce, tough tomatoes, and ho-hum toss-ins. In this chapter I have assembled an interesting mix of flavors, textures, colors, and combinations. They range from the simple and interesting flavors of the Fennel and Green Bean Salad to the many-vegetable, complex flavors of Caponata. I like to spread either version of the Caponata on a slice of grilled or toasted Italian bread and often serve it as an appetizer to my cooking-school students to take the edge off their hunger when they come to school directly from work.

When tomatoes are at peak flavor, the Bread and Chick-Pea Salad is a frequent visitor to my table. The White Bean Chicken Salad can be doubled easily and used as part of an antipasto table for a party. Ditto for the Bean and Tuna Salad with Radicchio and the Fennel and Green Bean Salad.

You'll notice a preponderance of beans in my salad recipes, and that's a thoroughly Italian touch. Cooks in Italy appreciate the texture and "meaty" flavor that beans add to salads—from the white cannellini to the firm chick-pea to the delicate lentil—and have always taken full advantage of the economical and versatile legume. And for those of you in search of light meals, these hearty mixtures make a satisfying main dish accompanied by bread and perhaps fresh fruit for dessert. (For more entree salads, see the "Cold Pasta Salads" chapter.)

SALADS

Fennel

There are two types of fennel: the heading type, which produces the herb or seed (sometimes called *dried fennel*), and the bulbous type, which is the vegetable and the type used in the recipes throughout this book.

This wonderfully aromatic vegetable goes by several names: finocchio, sweet anise, Florentine fennel. Its anise flavor is particularly appealing, and cooked fennel is a wonderful accompaniment to any type of pork dish, but its versatility extends further. It can be eaten raw—thinly sliced and simply dressed with olive oil and lemon juice or made into a salad with, say, orange segments and olives.

Fennel is available year-round. When buying, press on the bulb part—it should be firm and compact. Note that there should be no spreading at the top of the bulb; this would indicate that the fennel is too old. Also, there should be no brown or rusty edges.

Insalata di Fagiolini al Finocchio

(Fennel and Green Bean Salad)

The pleasant anise flavor of fresh fennel works nicely with a simple dressing of olive oil, lemon, and a touch of garlic. Green beans and chopped tomatoes add the final touch of flavor and texture.

....

1. Trim the beans and cut them in half crosswise. Blanch the beans in boiling water until they are tender but still crisp, 4 to 5 minutes. Drain the beans and plunge them into cold water. Drain again and reserve.

2. Cut off the fennel stalk and the feathery green sprigs just above the bulb. Reserve some sprigs for a garnish. Pull off and discard outer layer of the bulb. Slice the bulb in half lengthwise and cut away the core. Cut the halves into quarters and slice the layers lengthwise into 1/4-inch slices.

3. Combine the beans, fennel, and tomatoes in a bowl. Set aside.

4. In a measuring cup, combine the lemon juice, olive oil, garlic, salt, and pepper. Stir well. Add the dressing to the vegetables and toss gently. Arrange the salad on a platter and garnish with fennel sprigs. The salad can be refrigerated up to 1 hour before serving, but bring it back to room temperature to serve it.

½ pound fresh green beans
1 medium size fennel bulb (about 4–5 ounces)
4 plum tomatoes, seeded and chopped
2 tablespoons fresh lemon juice
⅓ cup extra-virgin olive oil
1 clove garlic, put through a press
⅛ teaspoon salt
⅛ teaspoon freshly ground black pepper

Serves 6 to 8
Calories: 95 per serving

Insalata di Lenticchie e Radicchio

(Lentil and Radicchio Salad)

A do-ahead salad should you prefer, since the salad actually benefits from an hour or so of sitting at room temperature. While beans are much more popular in many parts of Italy, lentils give this salad a unique texture.

....

5 cups water
½ teaspoon salt
2 cups dried red lentils
½ cup extra-virgin olive oil
2 tablespoons balsamic
   vinegar
1 teaspoon finely chopped
   garlic
1 teaspoon dried oregano,
   crumbled
½ teaspoon freshly ground
   black pepper
salt to taste
1 cup (1 small radicchio)
   shredded radicchio
1 rib celery, chopped fine
½ cup finely chopped red
   onion
Radicchio cups for serving

1. In a saucepan or small pot, bring the water to a boil, add the salt and lentils, and simmer for 6 minutes. Remove the pan from the heat and let the lentils soak in the water for 5 to 6 minutes, until soft. Drain and reserve.

2. In a large salad bowl, whisk together the oil, vinegar, garlic, oregano, and pepper. Season with salt.

3. Add the radicchio, celery, and onion and toss lightly with the dressing. Add the reserved lentils; toss gently and thoroughly. The salad can be refrigerated for up to 1 hour. Serve at room temperature in individual radicchio cups.

Serves 6 to 8
Calories: 290 per serving

Caponata I

(Vegetable Stew I)

A classic Sicilian dish similar to the French ratatouille, caponata is best if it sits in the refrigerator for 1 day, after which it should sit at room temperature for about 1 hour. Serve it warmed as a side dish or slightly chilled as an appetizer with crusty Italian bread. The fennel in the second version adds an anise flavor, which makes it particularly suitable as a side dish with pork.

....

1. Trim and peel the eggplant; cut into 1-inch cubes. Put the eggplant in a bowl and sprinkle it with the salt. Place a dish and a heavy can or jar over the eggplant as a weight, then let the eggplant sit for about 45 minutes to drain it of its bitter liquid.

2. Run water into the bowl to rinse the eggplant thoroughly. Blot the eggplant between double layers of paper towels to dry.

3. In a large pot, warm the oil over medium-high heat. Add the celery, onion, and garlic and sauté for 2 minutes. Add the eggplant and sauté for 4 minutes (do not add more oil).

4. Add the tomatoes, breaking them up with the back of a wooden spoon. Cook, uncovered, at a low simmer until the liquid has reduced and the mixture is well blended— about 10 minutes.

5. Add the capers, parsley, olives, vinegars, sugar, and pine nuts. Add salt and pepper to taste. Cook, uncovered at a low simmer until there is little liquid left in the pan. Cool at room temperature for 30 minutes. Refrigerate tightly covered until ready to serve. Keeps for 1 week in the refrigerator.

2 firm eggplants (about 1 pound each)
2 tablespoons salt
½ cup virgin olive oil
½ cup diced celery with a few leaves
½ cup diced red onion
1 clove garlic, chopped fine
2 28-ounce cans plum tomatoes, drained
2 tablespoons drained capers, rinsed
2 tablespoons finely chopped flat-leaf parsley
¼ pound black olives, preferably oil-cured, pitted and chopped
¼ pound green olives, preferably oil-cured, pitted and chopped
2 tablespoons red wine vinegar
3 tablespoons balsamic vinegar
1 tablespoon sugar
¼ cup pine nuts
Black pepper to taste

Serves 10 to 12
Calories: 197 per serving

SALADS

Caponata II

(Vegetable Stew II)

In this thoroughly modern version of caponata I roast the vegetables that ordinarily would be sautéed or fried, which results in a lower fat and calorie count than Vegetable Stew I. Also I add fresh fennel and herbs, two ingredients not ordinarily found in caponata.

For ease of preparation, I have broken the recipe into four distinct cooking segments, each of which can be done ahead.

....

1 pound firm eggplant, peeled and cut into 1-inch cubes

2 medium-size (10- to 12-ounce) green bell peppers, cored, seeded, and chopped

6 ounces (1 medium-size bulb) trimmed fresh fennel bulb, chopped coarse

1 tablespoon virgin olive oil or olive oil spray

½ teaspoon freshly ground black pepper

1 tablespoon fresh thyme leaves or 1 teaspoon dried, crumbled

1 teaspoon dried oregano, crumbled

1 teaspoon coarse salt

1. Preheat the oven to 450°F. Put the eggplant, peppers, and fennel on a baking sheet or pizza pan. Drizzle the olive oil over the vegetables (or spray lightly). Sprinkle the pepper, herbs, and salt evenly over the vegetables. Roast for 10 to 12 minutes, turning once, until the vegetables are just cooked through. Set aside.

....

½ cup coarsely chopped celery

½ cup coarsely chopped red onion

¾ cup (about 6 ounces) sliced fresh mushrooms

2. Poach the celery in boiling water. After 1 minute, add the onion and mushrooms and poach for 2 minutes longer. Drain and set aside.

3. In a serving bowl large enough to hold all the ingredients, combine the olives, capers, pine nuts, and tomato puree. Set aside.

½ cup chopped oil-cured black olives
½ cup chopped green olives, preferably oil-cured
1 tablespoon drained capers, rinsed
¼ cup pine nuts
2½ cups tomato puree

4. In a small saucepan over medium-high heat, boil the vinegar and sugar for 2 minutes, stirring constantly. Remove from the heat to cool slightly.

½ cup red wine vinegar
2 teaspoons sugar
Salt and freshly ground black pepper to taste

5. To the serving bowl, add the roasted eggplant mixture and the celery and mushroom mixture. Stir well to combine. Add the vinegar reduction and combine well. Season with salt and pepper. The caponata will keep in the refrigerator for 4 or 5 days.

Serves 6 to 8
Calories: 171 per serving

Palermo-Style Seafood Caponata: In step 5, add 2 6- to 7-ounce cans water-packed tuna, drained.

SALADS

Insalata di Pollo e Fagioli

(White Bean Chicken Salad)

Beans and chicken would be an unusual combination in Italy, but they are a natural taste alliance. It is the savory parsley sauce that makes this one of my favorite salads—any time of the year.

....

2 pounds skinless chicken
   breasts
1 bay leaf
1 19-ounce can cannellini
   beans, drained and rinsed

PARSLEY DRESSING
1 cup flat-leaf parsley leaves
   and stems
2 cloves garlic, peeled
½ teaspoon salt
3 tablespoons extra-virgin
   olive oil
2 tablespoons red wine vinegar
2 tablespoons freshly grated
   Parmesan cheese
1 teaspoon dried oregano,
   crumbled
Freshly ground black pepper
   to taste
Leaf lettuce for serving

1. Put the chicken breasts in a pot with cold water to cover. Add the bay leaf. Bring the water to a boil and poach the breasts until they are cooked through—15 to 20 minutes. Remove the chicken from the water and allow to cool. Pull the meat from the bones and cube the meat.

2. Put the chicken and beans in a salad bowl and toss gently to combine.

3. Place all the dressing ingredients in a food processor fitted with the steel blade and process with short pulses until well combined. Add the dressing to the chicken and beans and toss gently to combine.

4. Arrange individual portions of the salad on leaf lettuce to serve. Or refrigerate for up to 2 hours before serving.

Serves 4
Calories: 400 per serving

Insalata di Ceci e Peperoni

(A Salad of Chick-Peas and Peppers)

It doesn't get much easier than this, but don't let that lull you into thinking that this dish might lack pizzazz. The texture of the chick-peas and the assertive flavor of the peppers combine two economical staples of my mother's kitchen—the chick-peas as an alternative to the ubiquitous beans, the peppers plucked from the garden and freshly roasted.

....

1. In a medium-size salad bowl, combine the chick-peas, red peppers, scallion, garlic, and basil. Add the olive oil and lemon juice; toss gently and thoroughly. Season with salt and pepper.

2. Refrigerate, covered, for at least 1 hour before serving. The salad can be made 1 day ahead; cover and refrigerate.

Serves 6 to 8
Calories: 145 per serving

2 15½-ounce cans chick-peas, drained and rinsed
1 7-ounce jar roasted red peppers, drained and sliced into strips
⅓ cup thinly sliced scallion
2 teaspoons finely chopped garlic
¼ cup chopped fresh basil
¼ cup extra-virgin olive oil
2 tablespoons fresh lemon juice
Salt and freshly ground black pepper to taste

Insalata di Pomodori Secchi e Fagioli

(A Salad of Sun-Dried Tomatoes and Beans)

This cool salad literally bursts with a kaleidoscope of flavors highlighting two very popular foods of northern Italy: sun-dried tomatoes and beans. The vegetables can be combined and refrigerated for an easy make-ahead dish.

....

½ cup thinly sliced celery
½ cup thinly sliced carrot
½ cup chopped red onion
½ cup thinly sliced drained oil-packed sun-dried tomatoes
1 19-ounce can cannellini beans, drained and rinsed
¼ cup chopped flat-leaf parsley
½ cup extra-virgin olive oil
2 tablespoons red wine vinegar
2 small cloves garlic, minced
8–10 fresh basil leaves (to taste), cut into thin strips
½ teaspoon salt
¼ teaspoon freshly ground black pepper
Leaf lettuce for serving

1. In a large bowl, combine the celery, carrot, onion, sun-dried tomatoes, beans, and parsley. Refrigerate while you prepare the dressing.

2. In a measuring cup, combine the olive oil, vinegar, garlic, basil, salt, and pepper and blend well. Let the dressing sit at room temperature for at least 30 minutes. Pour the dressing over the salad and toss gently. Refrigerate, covered, for at least 2 hours or overnight.

3. Place one or two leaves of leaf lettuce on individual serving plates and arrange the salad on top.

_____

Serves 4 to 6
Calories: 270 per serving

Sun-Dried Tomatoes

I rarely purchase sun-dried tomatoes that are packed in oil, because they are too expensive. All the sun-dried tomatoes used in my cooking school are purchased dried and then processed as follows: Put the dried tomatoes and a small yellow onion that has been quartered in a pot of boiling water. Boil for about 10 minutes, until the tomatoes are soft. Drain the liquid (you can strain it and save it to use as a flavoring for soups and sauces) and discard the onion. When cool enough to handle, spread the tomatoes on paper toweling to dry, blotting excess moisture.

Now the tomatoes can be packed (not too tightly) in jars and the jars filled with olive oil—just to cover the tomatoes. Store the jar in a cool place away from sunlight. Use the tomatoes directly from the jar in recipes that call for sun-dried tomatoes. Also, the olive oil can be used for cooking purposes or in a salad dressing.

If I wish to add flavor to the tomatoes, I add 2 or 3 whole cloves of garlic, which I remove and discard after no more than 6 days.

Fagioli e Tonno con Radicchio

(Bean and Tuna Salad with Radicchio)

Florentines favor white beans like no other Italians. Many of the classic preparations are nothing more than beans with, say, olive oil, pepper, and a leaf of sage. In this version of an Italian bean salad I use water-packed tuna instead of oil-packed to cut down on the calories, and I add coarsely chopped radicchio for texture, taste, and color. If you have the time, spread the drained and washed beans on paper towels to allow them to dry for about 30 minutes, to make the bean flavor more pronounced and to cut down excess moisture.

....

1 19-ounce can cannellini
   beans, drained and rinsed
1 cup (about 1 small head)
   coarsely chopped radicchio
¼ cup chopped red onion
2 tablespoons chopped flat-
   leaf parsley
1 6½-ounce can water-packed
   tuna, drained
¼ cup extra-virgin olive oil
1 tablespoon fresh lemon juice
1 tablespoon balsamic vinegar
½ teaspoon salt
3–4 grinds of black pepper

1. In a medium-size salad bowl, combine the beans, radicchio, onion, parsley, and tuna. Toss gently to combine.

2. Whisk together the olive oil, lemon juice, and vinegar until completely blended. Add the salt and pepper to taste. Drizzle the dressing over the salad and toss gently. The salad can be refrigerated for up to 1 hour before serving.

Serves 4
Calories: 278 per serving

Panzanella con Ceci

(Bread and Chick-Pea Salad)

Attributed to Tuscan peasants, this dish makes a simple single-dish summer meal that in recent years has grown in stature and popularity. The secret of its success is the bread; if it is not coarse and quite stale, it will absorb too much water. If you can get the dry Italian ring bread called *friselle*, use it for even better results. Panzanella can be served as an antipasto or a salad course.

....

1. Soak the bread in a bowl of cold water for 15 minutes. Remove it from the bowl and squeeze it well with your hands.

2. In a large serving bowl, combine the bread, tomatoes, capers, onion, celery, and chick-peas. Set aside.

3. In a food processor fitted with the steel blade, combine the parsley, garlic, oregano, and vinegar. Process for 15–20 seconds to combine. With the machine running, add the olive oil in a steady stream and process until smooth. Drizzle the dressing over the salad, add the basil, and toss well to combine. Season with the salt and pepper to taste. Allow the salad to sit at room temperature for 45 minutes to an hour before serving.

Serves 4 to 6
Calories: 269 per serving

3 cups ½-inch cubes 2- or 3-day-old Italian bread
1 pound (8–10) very ripe plum tomatoes, cut into ½-inch chunks
1 tablespoon drained capers
½ cup finely chopped red onion
½ cup finely chopped celery
1 cup drained canned chick-peas, rinsed
10 sprigs flat-leaf parsley
1 clove garlic, peeled
1 teaspoon dried oregano, crumbled
2 tablespoons balsamic vinegar
½ cup extra-virgin olive oil
8–10 leaves fresh basil (to taste), torn
½ teaspoon salt
4–5 grinds of black pepper

To Toast Pine Nuts

Place a teaspoon of olive oil in a skillet (preferably nonstick) set over medium heat. Add the pine nuts in one layer and cook and stir until they just begin to turn toasty brown. Stay with the process, because once the heat starts to toast the pine nuts they turn very quickly and it is easy to burn them. Remove the pan from the heat and transfer them at once to a plate or bowl.

If I stretch the point a bit, I could say that the Italian frittata is very similar to the French or American omelet. But the frittata is usually served at the lighter evening meal, is cooked differently, takes on a different shape, and can be served hot or cold. The only link to the omelet is the use of eggs along with various fillings or flavoring ingredients.

In all of the frittata recipes I use an egg substitute—liquid eggs—that cuts down on most of the fat and cholesterol without affecting the flavor of the finished dish. I tested these recipes with several brands of liquid eggs and found practically no difference in flavor from one to another, so use whatever brand is most convenient (some come frozen; some are in the refrigerated section of supermarkets).

Several tips for making and serving successful frittate:

- A frittata must be cooked over low heat, very slowly; it should not be rushed.
- Do not overbrown the bottom, or it will change the otherwise appetizing appearance.
- Before you put the first ingredient in the frying pan, preheat the broiler and move the oven rack to within 4 to 5 inches of the heat element. By leaving the oven door open you can leave the handle of the omelet pan sticking out so it doesn't get exposed to the heat.

FRITTATE

- Use a nonstick omelet or frying pan.

- Prepare all the ingredients ahead—washing, chopping, dicing, and so forth.

- All a frittata needs as an accompaniment is crusty Italian bread and, if served as an evening meal, a simple green salad.

- Use zero-fat, zero-cholesterol liquid eggs and you can enjoy frittate with zero guilt.

- One cup of liquid eggs is roughly equivalent to four whole eggs.

Frittata Verdure

(Vegetable Omelet)

....

1. Preheat the broiler. In an 8-inch nonstick omelet pan, warm the oil over low heat. Add the mushrooms and sauté for 2 to 3 minutes or until the mushrooms release their moisture. Add the broccoli, zucchini, and scallion and cook for 2 minutes.

2. Put the eggs in a glass measuring cup and stir in the salt and pepper. Pour the eggs into the pan. Crumble the thyme over the eggs. As the frittata cooks, run a knife between the edge of the frittata and the pan, tilt the pan slightly, and let the eggs trickle to the edge. When the bottom of the frittata is set, in 3 to 4 minutes, sprinkle the Parmesan cheese over the top and move the pan from the stove to the preheated broiler, the oven rack set 4 to 5 inches from the heat, the handle of the omelet pan sticking out, away from the heat.

3. Leave the pan under the broiler only until the top is set but not dry, 1 to 2 minutes. Remove the pan from the broiler and run a knife around the edge of the frittata to loosen it. Place a plate over the pan and invert the frittata onto the plate.

Serves 1
Calories: 186 per serving

2 teaspoons virgin olive oil or olive oil spray
¼ cup (about 2 ounces) sliced fresh mushrooms
¼ cup cooked small broccoli florets
2 tablespoons diced zucchini
1 tablespoon chopped scallion
½ cup no-fat liquid eggs
Pinch of salt
2–3 grinds of black pepper
¼ teaspoon dried thyme, crumbled
1 tablespoon freshly grated Parmesan cheese

Pasta Frittata

(Pasta Omelet)

....

2 ounces linguine, vermicelli,
   or thin spaghetti
1 tablespoon virgin olive oil or
   olive oil spray
¾ cup chopped fresh plum
   tomatoes
½ teaspoon minced garlic
1 cup no-fat liquid eggs
Pinch of salt
2–3 grinds of black pepper
2 tablespoons freshly grated
   Parmesan cheese
2 tablespoons finely torn fresh
   basil or ½ teaspoon dried,
   crumbled

1. In a pot of boiling salted water, cook the pasta until it is almost al dente. Transfer the pasta to a bowl of warm water and set aside.

2. Preheat the broiler. In a 10-inch nonstick omelet pan set over medium heat, warm the oil for 1 minute. Add the tomatoes and the garlic and sauté for about 3 minutes or until the tomatoes soften slightly. Transfer the tomatoes to a small bowl.

3. Reduce the heat to low. Lift the cooked pasta out of the water and distribute it evenly over the bottom of the omelet pan. Put the pan back on the heat and spread the tomatoes evenly over the pasta.

4. Put the eggs in a measuring cup and stir in the salt and the pepper. Pour the eggs over the pasta and tomatoes. Sprinkle on the Parmesan cheese. As the frittata cooks, run a knife between the edges of the frittata and the pan, tilting the pan slightly to let the eggs trickle to the edge. When the bottom of the frittata is set, in 3 to 4 minutes, move the pan from the stove to the preheated broiler with the oven rack set 4 to 5 inches from the heat, the handle of the omelet pan sticking out, away from the heat.

5. Leave the pan under the broiler until the top is set but not dry, about 2 minutes. Remove the pan from the broiler and run a knife between the pan and the frittata to loosen it. Place a serving plate over the omelet pan and invert the pan to release the frittata onto the plate. Sprinkle the basil evenly over the top. Cut the frittata in half or into wedges and serve.

Serves 2
Calories: 258 per serving

Frittata con Pane e Peperoni

(Omelet with Bread and Peppers)

....

2 tablespoons virgin olive oil
or olive oil spray
¾ cup chopped green bell
pepper
3–4 ⅛-inch-thick slices day-
old Italian or French bread
to fit snugly into a 10-inch
omelet pan
1 cup no-fat liquid eggs
Pinch of salt
¼ teaspoon freshly ground
black pepper
10–12 sliced rounds of plum
tomatoes
1 teaspoon dried oregano,
crumbled
1 tablespoon freshly grated
Parmesan cheese

1. Preheat the broiler. In a 10-inch nonstick omelet pan, warm the oil over medium heat for 1 minute. Add the peppers and sauté until the peppers begin to soften, about 3 to 4 minutes. Transfer the peppers to a plate and reserve.

2. Reduce heat to low. Fit the bread into the omelet pan and put it back on the heat.

3. Put the eggs in a measuring cup and stir in the salt and pepper.

4. Pour the eggs into the pan over and around bread. Spread reserved peppers evenly on the top. As frittata cooks, run a knife between the edges of the pan and frittata, tilting pan slightly to let eggs trickle to the edge. When the bottom of the frittata is set and somewhat firm, in 3 to 4 minutes, arrange the sliced tomatoes evenly over the top. Sprinkle with oregano and cheese and transfer pan to preheated broiler with oven rack set 4 to 5 inches from the heat, the handle of the pan sticking out, away from heat.

5. Leave the pan under the broiler until the top is set but not dry, about 2 minutes. Remove the pan from the broiler and run a knife around the edges of the frittata. Tap the bottom of the pan lightly against the edge of the kitchen counter or on a chopping board to ensure the easy release of the frittata. Slide the frittata, tomato side up, onto a serving plate. Cut into four wedges and serve.

Serves 2
Calories: 247 per serving

FRITTATE

Frittata con Spinaci

(Spinach Omelet)

....

1. Preheat the broiler. In a 10-inch nonstick omelet pan, warm the olive oil and butter over low heat for 1 minute. Add the spinach to the pan. It will look like too much for the pan; press it down and cover the pan. After a few minutes the spinach will have wilted; remove the cover and leave it off.

2. Put the eggs in a measuring cup and stir in the pepper. Pour the eggs into the pan. As the frittata cooks, run a knife between the frittata and the edges of the pan, tilting it slightly to let the eggs trickle to the edge. Add the cheese and press it lightly into the frittata with your fingers. When the bottom of the frittata is set, in 3 to 4 minutes, move the pan from the stove to the preheated broiler with the oven rack set 4 to 5 inches from the heat, the handle of the omelet pan sticking out, away from the heat.

3. Leave the pan under the broiler until the top is set but not dry, about 2 minutes. Remove the pan from the broiler and run a knife between the pan and the frittata to loosen it. Place a serving plate over the omelet pan and invert the pan to release the frittata onto the plate. Cut in half or into wedges and serve.

1 tablespoon virgin olive oil or olive oil spray
1 tablespoon unsalted butter
½ 10-ounce package fresh spinach, coarse stems removed
1 cup no-fat liquid eggs
⅛ teaspoon freshly ground black pepper
1 cup grated part-skim mozzarella cheese

Serves 2
Calories: 316 per serving

Frittata con Patate e Peperoni

(Potato and Bell Pepper Omelet)

....

4 small (about ½ pound) red-
skinned potatoes

1 tablespoon virgin olive oil or
olive oil spray

1 cup chopped red or green
bell pepper or a
combination of both

1 cup no-fat liquid eggs

⅛ teaspoon dried rosemary,
crumbled

⅛ teaspoon freshly ground
black pepper

1. In a saucepan of boiling water, boil the potatoes until they are tender but not soft, 8 to 10 minutes. When cool enough to handle, peel the potatoes and dice them. You will need about 1 cup.

2. Preheat the broiler. In a 10-inch nonstick omelet pan or skillet, warm the oil over low heat for 1 minute. Add the peppers and stir to coat them with the oil. Cover the pan and sweat the peppers for 3 minutes. Uncover the pan and add the potatoes. Stir and cook until the potatoes just start to take on some color, about 3 to 4 minutes.

3. Put eggs in a measuring cup and stir in the rosemary and pepper. Pour eggs into the pan. Push the potatoes around to allow the eggs to even out. As the frittata cooks, run a knife between the edges of the frittata and the pan, tilting the pan slightly to let the eggs trickle to the edge. When the bottom of the frittata is set, 3 to 4 minutes, move the pan to the preheated broiler, the oven rack set 4 to 5 inches from the heat, the handle of the pan sticking out, away from the heat.

4. Leave the pan under the broiler until the top is set but not dry, about 2 minutes. Remove the pan from the broiler and run a knife between the pan and the frittata to loosen it. Place a plate over the omelet pan and invert the pan to release frittata onto the plate. Cut in half or into wedges and serve.

Serves 2
Calories: 206 per serving

FRITTATE

Focaccia

Just about every region in Italy, and even towns within each region, has its own style and shape of focaccia. In fact, the pizza we're familiar with today evolved from focaccia, the focaccia "toppings" at that point in time being nothing more than olive oil and herbs. As the evolution continued, tomatoes were added (16th century), and then cheese (1889), and so pizza came to be.

Every region in Italy has some type of focaccia that is used as daily bread. In the Liguria region the bread is infused with the flavors of olive oil and fresh basil. In Calabria the bread is stuffed with tomatoes or salt cod (baccalà) or mozzarella. A Neapolitan favorite is focaccia stuffed with eggs in their shells.

Focaccia is simply a flat bread—a table bread that can be used to accompany any meal or any dish—that in its purest form has nothing more than dimples, made by inserting fingers into the dough before baking, across the top. One reason for the popularity of focaccia is that it can be flavored with any number of ingredients—a combination of herbs (fresh or dried), for example.

The dough for making a basic focaccia is nothing more than flour, yeast, salt, water, and olive oil—not much different from pizza dough. The difference, of course, is that the dough for focaccia is thicker—breadlike actually—which increases its versatility, as it can be sliced horizontally and grilled for making a bruschetta. Sometimes I cut a round bruschetta horizontally and make a sandwich with roasted peppers or sun-dried tomatoes, olives, and thin slices of provolone cheese. I then cut the sandwich into wedges and serve it for lunch or put it on a buffet.

Focaccia can be shaped into an oval, as in Flat Bread with Fennel, or it can be round or rectangular. It is this versatility—in shape, size, and flavorings—that makes focaccia so popular.

Rubbing or brushing a small amount of olive oil across the top of the dough before baking will give the finished product a darker color.

Once the focaccia has cooled, it can be wrapped and frozen if desired.

Note that I've specified instant (quick-rise) yeast where it greatly improves the results of the recipe, but feel free to use it in the other recipes if you wish to speed the rising process.

Pizza

The popularity of pizza is well known, but it has only been in recent years that the idea of healthy pizza has caught on. Many restaurants today are serving cheeseless pizza and vegetarian pizza. In fact, my recipe for Greengrocer's Pizza is an adaptation of those being served at several restaurants in Chicago; it is great for a light summer luncheon, and in smaller portions makes an interesting first course or late-night snack. My New Wave Pizza is a style of pizza that has come into its own only in recent years, but it fits the eating styles of today where flavor and healthy eating are both important. The end result is that you can have your pizza and enjoy it without feeling guilty.

I grew up next to an Italian bakery that every summer would make pizza for many of the resorts in the "Italian Alps" section of the Catskill Mountains in upstate New York. In my mind's eye I can still see those magnificent pizze that were assembled and baked in large black rectangular pans. The thick dough was topped with a basil- and oregano-seasoned puree made from fresh tomatoes. Chopped fresh garlic was strewn over the tomatoes, followed by a heavy dusting of grated Romano cheese. The final taste fillip was a drizzle of olive oil. These pizze knocked me out; the fragrance of the herbs and oil, the taste, the fresh-baked smell. This was some kind of pizza, but we didn't call it pizza; we called it "tomato pie."

But having an Italian bakery next door that made pizza as a sideline did not deter my mother from making pizza from scratch every Saturday. The pizza she made was a more traditional round New York–style pizza (thick-crust edge; thin through the center). I know this: As many pizze as she would make, we—my father, my three brothers and I—would polish off, as Mom made pizza that was even better than the bakery pizza.

So it is that I am still involved with pizza. I have learned a lot about this wonderful pie over the years. For example, if you wish, you can make your pizza dough the day before you plan to use it. Make the pizza dough as directed in the recipes that follow, let it rise for 1 hour, punch it down, ball it, place it back in the bowl, cover it with plastic wrap and a kitchen towel, and put it in the refrigerator. Two to three hours before you are ready to make pizza, take the dough out of the refrigerator, let it come to room temperature (it will rise again), and roll out the dough for your favorite pizza.

Using a baking stone (my original invention, circa 1973) to bake pizza definitely improves the crust and duplicates the hearth effect of a wood-burning oven, giving the pizza a crispy, nonsoggy crust.

If you are using cheese on your pizza, use part-skim mozzarella cheese; it cuts out a lot of fat, and it melts and browns better during the baking.

I offer here just a small sampling of pizze. Let your imagination run free when it comes to toppings. Use just about any combination of available vegetables. Fresh vegetables work better, but frozen vegetables such as broccoli and spinach are perfectly fine. Use generous amounts of fresh herbs, freshly sliced plum tomatoes, combine several types of fresh mushrooms (sauté them first in some olive oil and garlic) . . . there's no end to the versatility of pizza.

Focaccia con Finocchio

(Flat Bread with Fennel)

The addition of potato buds and nonfat dry milk to the dough results in a soft, yielding focaccia that has a pleasant chew. The fennel seed is finely ground (I use a small electric coffee grinder), so the subtle flavor of anise pervades the dough.

....

1 ¼-ounce package instant active dry yeast

1¼ cups very warm water (120–125°F)

1 teaspoon sugar

¼ cup potato buds (instant mashed potatoes)

1 tablespoon nonfat dry milk

1 tablespoon salt

4 cups unbleached all-purpose flour

2 teaspoons finely ground fennel seeds

1 tablespoon virgin olive oil

1. In a large mixing bowl or the bowl of a stand mixer, dissolve the yeast in ¾ cup of the water. Add the sugar, potato flakes, dry milk, and salt. Stir well to combine. Allow the mixture to sit for 10 minutes.

2. Add the flour, 1 cup at a time, stirring well to combine. Add the remaining ½ cup water and the fennel. Combine and mix well. Knead the dough on a lightly floured surface until it is smooth and satiny, not sticky—5 to 7 minutes. Form the dough into a ball and place it in a large mixing bowl. Rub the surface of the dough with 1 teaspoon of the olive oil. Cover the bowl with plastic wrap and then a kitchen towel and place in a warm spot (not an oven).

3. Let the dough rise until it has doubled in bulk, about 1½ hours. Punch down the dough and remove it from the bowl. Rub 1 teaspoon of olive oil across the bottom of a 12″ × 18″ cookie sheet or baking pan. Spread and press the dough into an oval shape about 15″ × 5″ × ½″. Cover the pan with a clean towel and let the dough rise for 30 minutes. Meanwhile, preheat the oven to 500°F. Brush or rub the top of the focaccia with the remaining teaspoon of olive oil and, with your fingers stiff, plunge two of them into the

dough, working from the center, to form holes that are about 2 inches apart.

4. Bake the focaccia on the middle rack of the oven for 10 minutes. Turn the oven down to 425°F and bake for an additional 10 to 15 minutes, until the top is dark brown and the focaccia is cooked through. Cool the focaccia on a wire rack. Wrap leftovers in plastic wrap and store at room temperature for 1 day.

Makes 1 focaccia of about 2 pounds, serving 8 to 10
Calories: 219 per serving

Focaccia al Pomodori Secchi

(Tomato and Garlic Flat Bread)

For this focaccia I use the sponge method of dough making. This gives the yeast a head start—time to feed on the flour—resulting in a light texture. Also, adding the garlic to the sponge mellows its flavor; just a subtle hint of garlic comes through. If you would like a stronger garlic flavor, double the amount.

....

SPONGE

1 ¼-ounce package active dry
   yeast
1 cup warm water (105–
   115°F)
1 cup unbleached all-purpose
   flour
2 cloves garlic, crushed

1. In a large mixing bowl, dissolve the yeast in the warm water. Add the flour and garlic and stir well. Cover the bowl and let the sponge sit for at least 1 hour and up to 2 hours.

....

DOUGH

3 cups unbleached all-purpose
   flour
1 tablespoon salt
⅛ teaspoon freshly ground
   black pepper
½ cup drained oil-packed
   sun-dried tomatoes patted
   dry and chopped coarse
2–3 tablespoons warm water

2. To the sponge, add the flour, salt, pepper, and sun-dried tomatoes. Mix and combine well. Add warm water as needed to make a dough that is firm, not sticky. Knead the dough on a lightly floured surface for 5 to 6 minutes, until it is smooth and satiny. Form the dough into a ball and place it in a lightly floured large bowl. Cover the bowl with plastic wrap and then a kitchen towel and place it in a warm place to rise for 1½ hours.

3. Preheat the oven to 450°F. Spread and press the dough into a lightly oiled 12-inch round baking pan that is 1 inch high. Smooth out the dough. Cover the pan and let the dough rise for 30 minutes. With stiff fingers, punch holes in the top of the dough using two

fingertips. Bake the focaccia for 25 to 30 minutes, until dark brown and cooked through.

4. Cool on a wire rack. Wrap leftovers in plastic wrap and store at room temperature for 1 day.

Serves 6 to 8
Calories: 255 per serving

Variations: To make smaller focaccae, cut the dough into equal pieces and press it into 9- or 10-inch pans.

For a thicker, lighter finished focaccia, give the dough a longer second rise.

To the basic dough, any of the following can be added singly or in combination, but do not use more than three ingredients: ½ cup diced part-skim mozzarella; ½ cup oil-cured black olives, pitted and chopped coarse; a combination of crumbled dried herbs such as oregano, basil, rosemary—1 teaspoon each.

Pasta Base per la Pizza

(Pizza Dough)

This dough recipe will make two 14-inch pizza crusts for thin-crust pizza. If you plan to make only one pizza, make a tight round ball with the remaining dough (after it has had one rise), wrap it well, and freeze it for later use. (Let the frozen dough thaw overnight in the refrigerator when you're ready to make your pizza.) If you like a thicker crust, put half the dough on, say, a 12-inch pan.

If you measure the flour and water absolutely without variance, the recipe will work perfectly every time.

....

1 ¼-ounce package active dry yeast

1 cup plus 1 tablespoon warm water (105–115°F)

4 cups unbleached all-purpose flour

1 teaspoon salt

2 tablespoons virgin olive oil

1. In a small bowl, dissolve the yeast in ½ cup plus 1 tablespoon of the warm water and stir well. Set aside. Combine the flour and salt in a 3- to 4-quart mixing bowl. Make a well in the center of the flour. Add the olive oil to the yeast mixture, then add that to the flour. Add the remaining warm water, stir, and mix well until a rough mass of dough is formed and the dough cleans the sides of the bowl. If the dough is not soft and pliable, add 1 teaspoon warm water.

2. Turn the dough out of the bowl onto a lightly floured work surface. Knead the dough for 6 to 8 minutes, until smooth and soft. Lightly flour a round or rectangular pan with high sides (a lasagne pan works nicely). Divide the dough into two equal pieces. Working with one piece at a time, work the dough with both hands to form a tight ball. Place the balls of dough in the pan and lightly dust the top of each ball of dough with flour. Cover the pan with plastic wrap and then a kitchen towel. Set the pan in a warm place for the dough balls to rise until doubled in bulk, about 1½ hours.

3. After the dough has doubled in bulk, gently lift each ball from the pan, place it on a lightly floured surface, and roll it to the desired diameter. Transfer the dough to a lightly oiled flat pizza pan or a pizza screen. If necessary, the dough can take a short second rise, covered with a towel or plastic wrap to prevent drying, on the pan or screen; this will result in a pizza of lighter texture. Use the dough to make any of the following pizzas.

Makes 29 ounces of dough, enough for 2 14-inch pizzas, about 16 1-slice servings
Calories: 130 per serving

Pasta per la Pizza Integrale
(Whole-Wheat Pizza Dough)

This is a good departure from the standard white dough in that it adds color and a slightly different flavor to the baked pizza. Do not attempt to use all whole-wheat flour; it does not contain enough gluten to develop a usable dough.

....

1 ¼-ounce package active dry yeast
2 teaspoons honey
½ cup warm water (105– 115°F)
2 tablespoons virgin olive oil
3 cups unbleached all-purpose flour
1 cup whole-wheat flour
1 teaspoon salt
½ cup plus 1 tablespoon warm water

Follow the directions for making Pizza Dough (preceding recipe).

Makes 2 14-inch pizza crusts, about 16 1-slice servings
Calories: 130 per serving

Pizza dell 'Ortolano

(Greengrocer's Pizza)

A salad is tossed onto a baked pizza shell—a salad pizza pure and simple—with the rules bent a bit to add some cheese. This has become a very popular pizza in restaurants across the country in the last three or four years. The Italian title literally means "the greengrocer's pizza," so use your imagination in combining greens and vegetables for your own rendition.

....

1. Preheat the oven to 425°F. Make the salad and salad dressing. In a large salad bowl, combine the lettuces, onion, and tomatoes. Set aside. (Salad—without the dressing—can be made ahead and refrigerated for several hours.) In a small bowl, combine the olive oil, vinegar, and lemon juice. Whisk well to combine. Season with salt and pepper.

2. Place the pizza crust in a lightly oiled 14-inch pizza pan. Prick the surface deeply all over with a fork. Bake the crust on the lower rack of the oven for 10 to 12 minutes, until it turns toasty brown. (The recipe can be made to this point up to 2 hours ahead and held.) A few minutes before removing the pizza from the oven, lay slices of provolone evenly across the crust, except for the edges; bake until the cheese melts. Remove the pizza from the oven and set aside. Drizzle half or more of the salad dressing over the greens (you may have some left over, depending on how much dressing you like on your salad) and toss well. Lay the salad over the crust and serve.

6-7 cups mixed lettuces—red leaf, leaf, radicchio
¼ cup sliced red onion
6-7 tomatoes, cubed
½ cup extra-virgin olive oil
1 teaspoon balsamic vinegar
1 teaspoon fresh lemon juice
Salt and freshly ground black pepper to taste
1 14-inch pizza crust
6-8 thin slices provolone cheese, about 6 ounces

Makes 1 14-inch pizza, about 8 1-slice servings
Calories: 344 per serving

Pizza Vongole

(Clam Pizza)

The thyme and red pepper flakes are the seasonings that make this pizza zing with good flavor.

....

1 14-inch pizza crust
3 tablespoons virgin olive oil
2 6½-ounce cans minced clams, drained and juice reserved
2 tablespoons minced garlic
¼ teaspoon crushed red pepper flakes
3 tablespoons minced flat-leaf parsley
1 teaspoon dried thyme, crumbled

1. Preheat the oven to 425°F. Place the crust in a lightly oiled 14-inch pizza pan. Brush or rub the crust with 1 tablespoon of the olive oil. Distribute the clams evenly over the surface of the pizza. Add the garlic, red pepper flakes, parsley, and thyme. Drizzle the remaining 2 tablespoons oil over the pizza. Sprinkle on 4 or 5 tablespoons of the reserved clam juice.

2. Bake the pizza on the lower rack of the oven for 10 to 12 minutes, until the crust is brown and cooked through.

Makes 1 14-inch pizza, about 8 1-slice servings
Calories: 215 per serving

Pizza alla Moda

(New Wave Pizza)

This fashionable pizza incorporates myriad flavors, but just as enjoyable are the many textures that play a stylish tune up and down the taste buds. And if you're a fan of cold pizza, you'll really like this one.

....

1. Preheat the oven to 475°F. Place the pizza crust in a lightly oiled 14-inch pizza pan or on a lightly floured pizza peel. Add the toppings in the order listed, starting with the scallions and ending with the cheese. Drizzle the olive oil over the top of the pizza.

2. Bake the pizza on the lower rack of the oven or on a baking stone for 12 to 15 minutes, until the crust is brown and the cheese has melted.

Makes 1 14-inch pizza, about 8 1-slice servings
Calories: 275 per serving

1 14-inch pizza crust
6-7 scallions (to taste), white part and 1 inch of the green stalk, chopped
6-7 pencil-thin stalks asparagus (to taste), trimmed and cut into 1-inch pieces
3 small (about 6 ounces) red-skinned potatoes, sliced as thin as possible
3 ounces fresh mushrooms, sliced thin (about ⅓ cup)
1 teaspoon dried thyme, crumbled
1 teaspoon dried rosemary, crumbled
1 teaspoon crushed red pepper flakes
7 ounces provolone cheese, grated (about 2 cups)
2 tablespoons virgin olive oil

Pizza alle Verdure Arrostite

(Roasted Vegetable Pizza)

Roasting all the vegetables on the same pan not only saves a lot of work but also helps to blend the flavors without using a lot of extra cooking oil. You can roast the vegetables 2 to 3 hours ahead of time.

....

1 1-pound eggplant, peeled and cut into ½-inch cubes
¼ cup sliced scallions
1 pound (8–10) plum tomatoes, cut in half lengthwise, each half then cut into 4 pieces
1 cup chopped zucchini
1 teaspoon dried thyme, crumbled
1 teaspoon dried oregano, crumbled
4 cloves garlic, sliced thin (optional)
⅛ teaspoon freshly ground black pepper
⅛ teaspoon salt
3 tablespoons virgin olive oil
1 14-inch pizza crust
3 tablespoons freshly grated Parmesan cheese

1. Preheat the oven to 425°F. Put all of the vegetables on a 12″ × 18″ baking pan. Sprinkle on the thyme, oregano, and garlic. Add the pepper and salt. Toss to combine thoroughly. Drizzle on the olive oil and, using two large spoons, toss to coat the vegetables with the oil.

2. Roast the vegetables for 5 minutes. Remove the pan from the oven and toss the vegetables. Return the pan to the oven and roast for 5 minutes more. Remove the pan from the oven, but do not turn the oven off. Set the vegetables aside to cool for a few minutes.

3. Place the pizza crust in a lightly oiled 14-inch pizza pan. Spread all of the roasted vegetables evenly across the pizza crust. Sprinkle on the Parmesan cheese. Bake the pizza for 10 to 12 minutes, until the crust is brown. Serve at once.

Makes 1 14-inch pizza, about 8 1-slice servings
Calories: 213 per serving

Polenta

Polenta, though greatly removed from risotto in texture and appearance, equals it in versatility. Many distinct flavors can be wrought from basic polenta simply by adding different ingredients, sauces, and stocks. Indeed, polenta surpasses risotto in many ways in that it can be served directly from the cooking pot in all of its golden creamy goodness; it can be baked, grilled, molded and cut, or layered; or it can receive, say, a tasty marinara sauce or mushroom sauce . . . there are many opportunities to explore the taste and goodness of this grain dish, one that predates the Middle Ages.

There are several grades of cornmeal to consider in the process of making polenta, and some cooks suggest that a particular degree of coarseness should be chosen for various dishes.

Coarsely ground cornmeal, labeled "Polenta, Product of Italy" and "Polenta Tradition," is typically golden in color. Its texture does produce a finished product that is more authentically Italian than the finely ground cornmeal sold in supermarkets, so it should be sought out. However, I suggest that you can work with either fine or coarse cornmeal in the recipes that follow, and they will turn out just fine.

Also, if 20 minutes—the average time it takes to make polenta—is too long for your frame of mind, consider using a most acceptable substitute from

Italy: instant polenta. The recommended cooking time in this case is only 5 minutes. The brand I am most familiar with is Fattorie e Pandea, and I purchase it at Italian food stores and at selected supermarkets.

The classic method of preparing polenta calls for finishing it off with gobs of butter and cheese (or cheeses). I have, in most of the recipes that follow, done away with that part of the process, thus cutting down much of the fat and cholesterol, yet still maintaining a high level of flavor and enjoyment. For example, the first recipe uses skim milk to thin out the polenta. This is a perfectly good alternative, one that adds a certain amount of creaminess while bringing the polenta to the proper consistency.

There are only two techniques you need to know to make first-rate polenta. The cornmeal must be added to the water in a slow yet constant stream to avoid lumps. I find that a heatproof measuring cup works well. Hold the cup high enough above the steaming water to prevent it from affecting the flow of the cornmeal. Other than that, all it takes is a strong, steady stirring of 20 minutes. Trivial stuff, really, when one considers the delicious consequences that result.

Risotto

Risotto is rice cooked with broth until it is creamy and al dente. Though accurate, that simplified description does not do justice to one of the most satisfying dishes in the Italian repertory of cooking.

Risotto is an important dish in the Italian kitchen, one that is becoming increasingly popular in the United States—not only because it is delicious but also because it parallels pasta for versatility and nutrition. It can be served as a first course instead of pasta or as an entree and adapts well to many different kinds of flavor additions.

Risotto in a cookbook whose title proclaims "easy"? Yes. While it is true that in the classic method of risotto cookery the pot must be tended and stirred for about 20 minutes, the work is really not difficult or laborious. In fact students in my cooking school, after only one risotto cooking demonstration, get wildly excited about making it at home because they see how simple and easy risotto is to make.

However, in addition to the classic method of making risotto, there is a shortcut method, one used by restaurants, that doesn't cut down on the time but does eliminate much of the stirring. This alternate method is explained following the classic method.

Classic Method: The basic ingredients are unsalted butter (omitted in the recipes that follow), olive oil, onion, Italian rice, and some type of boiling stock—chicken, vegetable, or beef. The most critical ingredient is the rice. Arborio or Carnaroli rice is the best for risotto. The rice grains, which are round, short, and stubby, have the ability to absorb a great deal of liquid without losing their firmness, and that is what ultimately makes risotto so different from other rice dishes.

According to the classic method, the onion is cooked gently in the oil and butter. Next the rice is added and cooked and stirred to coat the grains with the oil and butter. Hot stock is added to the pot ½ cup at a time, stirring all the while; the medium-high heat causes the broth to bubble briskly, and in a few minutes the liquid will be absorbed completely by the rice. This is repeated with the remaining stock, another ½ cup added only after previous additions have been absorbed. The simmer of the risotto should be fairly high, with bubbles appearing over the surface. After 18 to 20 minutes of cooking, stirring, and adding stock, the rice should be tender but firm, creamy but not too thick—*all'onda* or "wavy" as Italians like to call it.

Alternate Method: The alternate method can be done in either of two ways, but the preparation begins in the same way as explained in individual recipes.

1. The rice is cooked—employing the classic method of adding stock or broth in small doses—but only for 10 minutes. The rice is then removed from the heat and set aside. At this point it can be refrigerated for 2 to 3 hours or set on the kitchen counter for up to an hour. When ready to be finished, the pot is put back on the stove, a cup of hot stock or broth is added, the rice is brought back to a slower simmer, stirring constantly, and the process of adding simmering stock in small quantities is continued until the rice is al dente. Be careful; the rice may take less time to cook than you expect using this method, so test for doneness often.

2. In this method, instead of adding ½ cup of stock at the outset, 2 cups of simmering stock, enough to cover the rice completely, are added all at once to the rice in the pot, and the rice is given a good stir. The secret to this method is to keep everything at a lively simmer. After 6 or 7 minutes, come back to the pot. The liquid will be reduced, and the rice will be very visible. Add 2 more cups of simmering stock and stir well. Come back after 6 or 7 minutes and add another cup of stock. At this point the rice will be within 5 to 6 minutes of being done. Test for perfect al dente after a few more

minutes of cooking. After cooking risotto this way once, you will have the timing down perfectly.

Risotto adapts to a wide range of flavor additions. Vegetables, seafood, certain types of cheeses, and selected meats can be added to a basic risotto. Some of these ingredients may require some advance cooking; this will be addressed in individual recipes.

As an alternative to the defatted homemade Chicken Stock (see Index), use lower-salt canned chicken broth. Vegetarians can choose either Vegetable Stock or Mushroom Stock (recipes follow).

Polenta e Fagioli

(Polenta and Beans)

In this recipe the polenta is cooked half on the stove and half in the oven. Once cooked, the polenta can be cut into squares and served hot from the oven with chicken or veal. Or, as I often do, eat it cold from the refrigerator the next day with a salad.

1. Preheat the oven to 400°F. In a 3- to 4-quart saucepan or pot, bring the water and salt to a steady simmer. Turn the heat to medium and immediately begin adding the cornmeal in a thin yet constant stream (a glass measuring cup works nicely). If the cornmeal is added too quickly, lumps will form; to get rid of them, push them against the sides of the pot with the back of a wooden spoon. Stir constantly while adding the cornmeal. Once all of the cornmeal has been added, add the olive oil. Continue to cook and stir for 20 minutes. Watch the heat; if it is too high, the polenta will stick to the bottom of the pan.

2. Add the beans and pepper to the pot and combine thoroughly. Pour the polenta into a nonstick 8-inch square baking pan. Smooth the top with the back of a spoon or a spatula. Sprinkle the cheese over the top. Bake the polenta for 10 minutes.

3 cups water
½ teaspoon salt
1 cup yellow cornmeal
2 tablespoons virgin olive oil
1 cup drained canned cannellini or Great Northern beans, rinsed
Freshly ground black pepper to taste
2 tablespoons freshly grated Parmesan cheese

Serves 4 to 6
Calories: 166 per serving

Polenta con Scampi

(Polenta with Shrimp)

In this recipe the flavor of the dish is enhanced not only by the shrimp but also by the red pepper flakes. If, like me, you sometimes enjoy a spicier dish, by all means add more red pepper. When I am in a fiery mood, I even add a dash or two of Tabasco sauce.

....

2 tablespoons extra-virgin
  olive oil
16 (about 1¼ pounds) jumbo
  shrimp, shelled and
  deveined
1 28-ounce can plum
  tomatoes, with juice
⅛ teaspoon crushed red
  pepper flakes
1 teaspoon dried thyme,
  crumbled
3 cups water
½ teaspoon salt
1 cup yellow cornmeal
½ cup skim milk

1. In a large skillet set over medium-high heat, warm the oil and sauté the shrimp for 2 minutes, turning them constantly. Add the tomatoes, red pepper flakes, and thyme. Bring the sauce to a steady simmer and cook, uncovered, for 20 to 25 minutes while preparing the polenta. The sauce can be made up to a day ahead and refrigerated. Bring it back to a steady simmer for 2 to 3 minutes before using it.)

2. In a 3- to 4-quart saucepan or pot, bring the water and salt to a steady simmer. Turn the heat to medium and immediately begin adding the cornmeal in a thin yet constant stream (a glass measuring cup works nicely). If the cornmeal is added too quickly, lumps will form; to get rid of them, push them against the sides of the pot with the back of a wooden spoon. Stir constantly while adding the cornmeal and continue to cook and stir for 20 minutes. Watch the heat; if it is too high, the polenta will stick to the bottom of the pan. Add the skim milk and cook and stir for 3 minutes more. At this stage the polenta should tear away from the sides of the pot, a sign that it is ready.

3. Pour the polenta into a large oval or round serving platter. Make a well in the center or a depression down the middle and pour in the sauce and shrimp. Serve at once as an entree.

Serves 4
Calories: 359 per serving

Polenta ai Due Formaggi

(Polenta with Two Cheeses)

3 cups water
½ teaspoon salt
1 cup yellow cornmeal
1 tablespoon virgin olive oil
2 tablespoons freshly grated
  Parmesan cheese
¼ pound Gorgonzola cheese,
  crumbled
Salt and freshly ground black
  pepper to taste

1. In a 3- to 4-quart saucepan or pot, bring the water and salt to a steady simmer. Turn the heat to medium and immediately begin adding the cornmeal in a thin yet constant stream (a glass measuring cup works nicely). If the cornmeal is added too quickly, lumps will form; to get rid of them, push them against the sides of the pot with the back of a wooden spoon. Stir constantly while adding the cornmeal. After all the cornmeal is added, add the olive oil. Continue to cook and stir for 20 minutes. Add the cheeses, then cook and stir for 3 to 5 minutes longer, until the polenta tears away from the sides of the pot. Season with salt and pepper.

2. Serve individual portions directly from the pot or pour the polenta into a serving bowl. As the polenta cools, it will set. To bring it back to a creamy consistency, add some hot water or hot chicken broth. Serve as a side dish.

Serves 4 to 6
Calories: 180 per serving

Peperoni Arrostiti col Ripieno di Polenta

(Peppers Stuffed with Polenta)

In this recipe the cooked polenta is stuffed into open halves of roasted bell peppers. The peppers can be roasted and peeled well ahead of time and set aside. On occasion I dress the top of the stuffed peppers with a tablespoon or so of marinara sauce. Serve this dish with any chicken or veal dish.

1. Preheat broiler. To roast the peppers, put pepper halves, cut side down, on a baking sheet and place it under the broiler until the skins start to turn black—about 7 minutes. Place peppers in a bowl and cover the bowl with plastic wrap. After 10 minutes, remove peppers and peel off charred skin. Set aside.

2. In a 2- to 3-quart saucepan, bring the water and a pinch of salt to a steady simmer. Turn heat to medium and immediately begin adding the cornmeal in a thin yet constant stream (a glass measuring cup works well). Stir constantly while adding cornmeal. If the cornmeal is added too quickly, lumps will form; to get rid of them, push them against the sides of the pot with the back of a spoon. Add the olive oil and continue to cook and stir for 20 minutes. Season with salt and pepper. Preheat the oven to 425°F.

3. Place the peppers, cut side up, back on the baking sheet. Fill each of the pepper halves with the polenta and sprinkle each with 1 teaspoon of the cheese. Bake the stuffed peppers for 7 minutes. Serve at once.

2 5- to 6-ounce green or red bell peppers, cored, cut in half lengthwise, and seeded
2 cups water
Salt to taste
½ cup yellow cornmeal
1 teaspoon virgin olive oil
Freshly ground black pepper to taste
4 teaspoons freshly grated Parmesan cheese

Serves 4
Calories: 99 per serving

Polenta con Spinaci

(Polenta with Spinach)

To enhance the flavor of the polenta, I substitute chicken broth for a portion of the water. In this recipe I choose to pour the polenta onto a round pizza pan. However, it can just as easily be poured into fancy molds (lightly oil them first) or a baking pan of your choosing. Serve with chicken or veal.

....

2½ cups water
1 cup Chicken Stock (see Index) or lower-salt canned chicken broth
1 cup yellow cornmeal
2 tablespoons virgin olive oil
1 teaspoon freshly ground black pepper
1 10-ounce package frozen chopped spinach, cooked, drained, and squeezed dry
⅛ teaspoon freshly grated nutmeg
2 tablespoons freshly grated Parmesan cheese

1. In a 3- to 4-quart saucepan, bring the water and stock to a steady simmer. Turn the heat to medium and immediately begin adding the cornmeal in a thin yet constant stream (a glass measuring cup works well). Stir constantly while adding the cornmeal. If the cornmeal is added too quickly, lumps will form; to get rid of them, push them against the sides of the pot with the back of a wooden spoon. Add the olive oil and continue to cook and stir for 20 minutes. Add the pepper, spinach, and nutmeg and cook and stir for 2 minutes.

2. Pour the polenta into a 12-inch-diameter pizza pan or a similar pan and spread and smooth it to an even thickness. (The polenta can be made up to this point and held for up to 2 hours.) Preheat the oven to 400°F. Sprinkle the cheese evenly across the top and bake for 7 minutes. Remove the polenta from the oven, let it sit for 5 minutes, and cut it into wedges or squares for serving.

Serves 4 to 6
Calories: 152 per serving

Variation: Omit the spinach and nutmeg and, after the polenta has been baked, cut it into strips or squares and grill it.

Polenta con Marinara

(Polenta with Marinara Sauce)

A quick, simple marinara sauce enhances the flavor of polenta dramatically. If you wish, poach 1 pound sweet Italian sausage in water for 10 minutes or until cooked through. Cut the sausage into 1-inch pieces and add to the sauce when you add the tomatoes. With the sausage this becomes a main dish.

....

1. Make the sauce. Warm the oil in a large skillet over medium heat. Add the onion and cook until it just begins to soften, 2 to 3 minutes. Add the garlic and parsley and cook for 2 minutes more. Add the tomatoes, salt, and pepper. Keep sauce at a steady simmer while you make the polenta, but if sauce starts to thicken too much, turn the heat to low.

2. In a 3- to 4-quart saucepan or pot, bring the water and salt to a steady simmer. Turn the heat to medium and immediately begin adding the cornmeal in a thin yet constant stream (a glass measuring cup works nicely). Stir constantly while adding the cornmeal. If the cornmeal is added too quickly, lumps will form; to get rid of them, push them against the sides of the pan with the back of a wooden spoon. Watch the heat; if it is too high, the polenta will stick to the bottom of the pan. Continue to cook and stir for 20 minutes. When the polenta is ready, it should tear away from the sides of the pot.

3. Pour the polenta into a large oval or round serving platter. Make a well in the center or a depression down the middle and pour in the marinara sauce. Serve at once.

2 tablespoons virgin olive oil
2 tablespoons chopped yellow onion
2 cloves garlic, minced
3 tablespoons chopped flat-leaf parsley
1 28-ounce can plum tomatoes, with juice
Salt and freshly ground black pepper to taste
3 cups water
½ teaspoon salt
1 cup yellow cornmeal

Serves 4 to 6
Calories: 154 per serving

POLENTA AND RISOTTO

Polenta al Sugo di Funghi

(Polenta with Mushroom Sauce)

A fragrant and woodsy mushroom sauce adds an earthy touch to the polenta. Serve with roast game such as quail or pheasant or with rabbit or venison.

....

1 ounce dried porcini or cèpes
3 tablespoons virgin olive oil
1 clove garlic, minced
½ cup dry red wine
1 cup canned plum tomatoes
    passed through a food mill
    or pureed lightly in a food
    processor
2 tablespoons flat-leaf parsley
Salt and freshly ground black
    pepper to taste
3½ cups water
½ teaspoon salt
1 cup yellow cornmeal

1. Make the mushroom sauce. Soak the porcini in warm water for 20 minutes. Remove them from the water but do not discard the water. Rinse the mushrooms briefly under cold running water and pat them dry with paper towels. Strain the reserved liquid through a double layer of paper towels and set aside. Warm the oil in a saucepan set over medium-high heat. Add the garlic and cook for only 1 minute (do not burn the garlic). Add the wine, turn up the heat, and simmer until the alcohol has evaporated. Add the tomatoes and parsley. Simmer the sauce only for the time it takes to make the polenta, and add the reserved porcini, including the strained soaking liquid, at the very end. Season with salt and pepper.

2. Preheat the oven to 425°F. Make the polenta. In a 3- to 4-quart saucepan or pot, bring the water and ½ teaspoon salt to a steady simmer. Turn the heat to medium and immediately begin adding the cornmeal in a thin yet constant stream (a glass measuring cup works nicely). Stir constantly while adding the cornmeal. If the cornmeal is added too quickly, lumps will form; to get rid of them, push them against the sides of the pot with the back of a wooden spoon. Cook and stir the polenta for 20 minutes, until it tears away from the sides of the pot.

3. Pour the polenta into a nonstick 10-inch square cake pan (a smaller size will make the polenta thicker; a larger size will result in a thinner polenta, so use whatever size pan you already have). Bake the polenta for 10 minutes. Cut it into individual squares or a traditional diamond shape. Dress each piece with some of the sauce and serve at once.

Serves 4 to 6
Calories: 168 per serving

Brodo Vegetale

(Vegetable Stock)

....

1 tablespoon unsalted butter
2 tablespoons virgin olive oil
½ cup scraped and chopped
    carrot
½ cup chopped celery
¼ cup chopped leek, white
    part only
¼ cup chopped scallion
8 sprigs flat-leaf parsley
10 peppercorns
10 cups water

1. Melt the butter with the oil in a large, heavy stockpot or saucepan over medium heat. Add the vegetables and sauté for 5 minutes. Add the parsley, peppercorns, and water and heat to a boil. Reduce the heat to low to maintain a steady simmer. Cook, uncovered, until reduced to about 2 quarts—about 1 hour.

2. Strain the stock through a sieve, pressing on the vegetables with a wooden spoon to extract the liquids. Discard the vegetables. The broth can be refrigerated, covered, for 3 to 4 days. Heat to boiling before using.

_____

Makes about 6 cups
Calories: 62 per 1-cup serving

Brodo di Funghi

(Mushroom Stock)

....

1. Preheat the oven to 375°F. Put a thin film of water in a roasting pan. Add the carrots, celery, onion, and garlic and roast the vegetables for about 45 minutes, until browned slightly. Meanwhile, soak the porcini in warm water for 10 minutes.

2. Put the 4 quarts of water and mushroom pieces in a large pot. Heat to boiling. Reduce the heat to a simmer. Add the browned vegetables, the softened porcini (including the strained soaking liquid), and the remaining ingredients.

3. Simmer the stock, uncovered, for 2 hours. Add water as necessary to maintain a constant level of liquid. Strain the stock through a fine-mesh strainer lined with a double layer of dampened cheesecloth or paper towels. Cool slightly. Refrigerate until ready to use.

2 large carrots, trimmed, scraped, and halved
2 stalks celery (with a few leaves), halved
1 medium-size yellow onion, peeled and quartered
6 cloves garlic, peeled
1 ounce dried porcini or cèpes
4 quarts cold water
2 pounds mushroom stems and pieces (cultivated, shiitake, or chanterelle)
10 sprigs flat-leaf parsley
2 teaspoons black peppercorns
¼ teaspoon dried thyme, crumbled
1 teaspoon salt

Makes about 3 quarts
Calories: 23 per 1-cup serving

Risotto alla Milanese

(Risotto in the Style of Milan)

This is the classic by which all risotto are measured. I have made but minor adjustments to the traditional recipe, which doesn't change the final taste all that much. The changes are these: the elimination of butter, a reduction in olive oil, and use of lower-salt canned chicken stock if homemade broth is not used. It can be served as a first course preceding an entree or as an accompaniment to *Ossobuco* (see Index).

....

3 tablespoons extra-virgin olive oil
½ cup chopped yellow onion
½ cup dry white wine
1 pound (2¼ cups) Arborio or other short-grain rice
5–6 cups Chicken Stock (see Index) or lower-salt canned chicken broth
Pinch of saffron threads soaked in water
¾ cup freshly grated Parmesan cheese

1. Heat the oil in a heavy 4- to 5-quart pan over medium heat. Add the onion and sauté slowly. When the onion has softened, in about 2 minutes, add the wine, increase the heat to medium-high, and cook and stir until the alcohol has evaporated—about 2 minutes. Add the rice and stir well to coat the rice with the liquid in the pan.

2. Reduce the heat to medium. Add the simmering stock, about ½ cup at a time, stirring constantly. Add more stock ½ cup at a time as it is absorbed. Continue until you have used about 5 cups of the stock. After about 18 minutes of cooking, test the rice; it should be almost ready—al dente. If it is too firm, continue adding the stock while stirring. Total cooking time should not exceed 20 minutes.

3. Off the heat, stir in the saffron (including the soaking water) and freshly grated Parmesan. The risotto should be wavy and creamy, not "tight." Add a small amount of stock or hot water to loosen the risotto if necessary. Serve at once in individual bowls.

Serves 4 to 6
Calories: 426 per serving

Risotto al Finocchi

(Risotto with Fennel)

Cooking tempers the anise flavor of fennel just enough to tame it and bring out its sweetness. I prepare this risotto dish more than any other.

....

1. Pull off the outer layer of each fennel bulb. Cut each bulb in half lengthwise and cut away the small triangular core. Cut the halves in half lengthwise once again and then slice them lengthwise into slivers. Blanch the fennel in boiling water for about 4 minutes, until slightly soft. Drain and reserve.

2. Heat oil in a heavy 4- to 5-quart pot over medium heat. Add the onion and sauté slowly. When onion has softened, in about 2 minutes, add the wine. Increase heat to medium-high. Cook and stir until the alcohol has evaporated. Add rice to the pot and stir well to coat the rice with the liquid. Reduce heat to medium. Add the simmering stock about ⅓ cup at a time, stirring constantly. Add additional stock, ½ cup at a time, as it evaporates. After 10 minutes, add the reserved fennel. Continue cooking until you have used about 5 cups of stock. After about 18 minutes, test the rice; it should be almost ready—al dente. If it is too firm, continue adding stock while stirring. Total cooking time should not exceed 20 minutes. Season with pepper.

3. Off heat, stir in Parmesan. Risotto should be wavy and creamy. If "tight," add a small amount of stock or hot water to loosen it. Serve at once. Garnish with fennel sprigs.

2 small (3- to 4-ounce) fennel bulbs, trimmed and chopped
2 tablespoons extra-virgin olive oil
½ cup chopped yellow onion
½ cup dry white wine
1 pound (2¼ cups) Arborio or other short-grain rice
5–6 cups simmering Chicken Stock, Vegetable Stock (see Index), or lower-salt canned chicken broth, simmering
Freshly ground black pepper to taste
¾ cup freshly grated Parmesan cheese
Fennel sprigs for garnish

Serves 4 to 6
Calories: 410 per serving

Risotto con Asparagi e Pignoli

(Risotto with Asparagus and Pine Nuts)

The simple but flavorful addition of asparagus to a basic risotto creates a fresh and colorful dish. Try to find pencil-thin asparagus; they look better and cook better.

....

½ cup pine nuts
1 pound asparagus
2 tablespoons extra-virgin
   olive oil
½ cup chopped yellow onion
1 clove garlic, crushed
1 pound (2¼ cups) Arborio
   or other short-grain rice
5–6 cups Chicken Stock,
   Vegetable Stock (see Index),
   or lower-salt canned chicken
   broth, simmering
Freshly ground black pepper
   to taste
¾ cup freshly grated
   Parmesan cheese

1. Toast the pine nuts in a nonstick skillet over medium heat until lightly browned, 3 to 4 minutes. Set aside. If the asparagus stalks are thin, just snap the ends off where they break naturally. If thick, also peel the stalk with a vegetable peeler. Cut the asparagus into ½-inch pieces and reserve.

2. Heat the oil in a heavy 4- to 5-quart pot over medium heat. Add the onion and the garlic and sauté slowly. When the onion has softened, in about 2 minutes, add the rice and stir well to coat it with the liquid in the pan.

3. Add the simmering stock or broth about ½ cup at a time, stirring constantly. Add additional broth ½ cup at a time, as it evaporates. After 10 minutes, add the reserved asparagus (see note). Continue adding stock and stirring until you have used about 5 cups. After about 18 minutes of cooking, test the rice; it should be almost ready—al dente. If it is a bit too firm, continue adding stock while stirring. Total cooking time should not exceed 20 minutes. Add the reserved toasted pine nuts and season with pepper.

4. Off the heat, stir in the Parmesan cheese. The risotto should be wavy and creamy, not "tight." Add a small amount of stock or hot water to loosen the risotto if necessary. Serve at once in individual bowls.

Note: If you are not sure about the asparagus
size and relative cooking time, prepare the
asparagus as directed and blanch it in boiling
water until it is just cooked through. In that
case, add it to the risotto just before the
Parmesan cheese.

Serves 4 to 6
Calories: 477 per serving

Risotto ai Frutti di Mare

(Seafood Risotto)

The stock or broth used in this dish is made by boiling the shells from the shrimp. This is a substantial risotto, so it should be served as a main course, preceded by a small salad or bruschetta (see Index) and followed by a fruit tart or fresh fruit.

....

½ pound bay scallops
¾ pound small shrimp
1 quart water
1 small yellow onion, sliced
1 teaspoon dried thyme, crumbled
8 sprigs flat-leaf parsley
2 tablespoons extra-virgin olive oil
½ cup chopped yellow onion
1 clove garlic, put through a press
½ cup dry white wine
1 pound (2¼ cups) Arborio or other short-grain rice

1. Rinse the scallops under cold water and refrigerate. Shell and devein the shrimp, reserving the shells, then refrigerate the shrimp.

2. Put the shrimp shells in a 2- or 3-quart saucepan with the water. Add the sliced onion, thyme, and parsley. Bring to a boil, then reduce the heat and simmer the stock, uncovered, for 1 hour. Strain the stock through a fine-mesh strainer lined with two layers of dampened cheesecloth or paper towels. Measure the stock and add water as needed to make 6 cups liquid. Put the stock back into the saucepan and bring to a steady simmer.

3. Heat the oil in a heavy 4- to 5-quart pan over medium heat. Add the chopped onion and the garlic and sauté slowly. When the onion has softened, in about 2 minutes, add the wine. Increase the heat to medium-high and cook and stir until the alcohol has evaporated—about 2 minutes. Add the rice to the pan and stir to coat the rice.

4. Reduce the heat to medium. Add the simmering stock, about ½ cup at a time, stirring constantly. Add additional stock ½ cup at a time as it evaporates. Continue to add stock while stirring until about 4 cups have

been used. After the rice has cooked for 14 minutes, stir in the reserved scallops and shrimp. Finish cooking the rice, adding stock and stirring, for 4 to 5 minutes. Test the rice; it should be just about ready—al dente. If it is too firm, continue adding stock while stirring. Total cooking time should not exceed 20 minutes. The risotto should be wavy and creamy, not "tight." Add a small amount of stock or hot water to loosen the risotto if necessary. Serve at once in individual bowls.

Serves 6
Calories: 416 per serving

Riso, Funghi, e Piselli

(Rice with Mushrooms and Peas)

This recipe gently bends the rules for risotto cookery in that long-grain rice replaces Arborio, and the taste elements of the dish are treated separately and brought together at the very end. Serve as a main course, preceded by a salad or a bruschetta (see Index), for a light lunch.

....

½ cup chopped yellow onion
2 tablespoons unsalted butter
1 cup long-grain rice
2 cups Chicken Stock (see Index) or lower-salt canned chicken broth
2 tablespoons extra-virgin olive oil
6 ounces fresh mushrooms, (about ¾ cup) sliced thin
1 clove garlic, minced
¼ cup dry white wine
2 tablespoons chopped flat-leaf parsley
½ cup frozen peas, soaked in hot water for 5 minutes
Salt and freshly ground black pepper to taste

1. In a saucepan over medium heat, cook the onion in the butter until it just begins to turn limp, 3 to 4 minutes. Stir in the rice and cook and stir for 1 minute to coat the rice. Add the stock, bring to a steady simmer, cover the pan, turn the heat to low, and cook for 18 to 20 minutes, until the rice is al dente.

2. While the rice is cooking, warm the oil in a skillet over medium heat. Add the mushrooms and garlic and cook, stirring, until the mushrooms release their moisture and turn golden brown—about 3 minutes. Add the wine, turn the heat to medium-high, and cook for 2 minutes. Add the parsley and peas and cook for 1 minute longer. Remove from the heat.

3. Combine the mushrooms and peas with the rice, season with salt and pepper, and serve at once in heated bowls.

Serves 4
Calories: 344 per serving

Vegetables

My most recent trip to Italy was spent in Emilia-Romagna, a region where the earth is so fertile that practically anything thrown in the ground grows. The bounty from those fertile fields shows up time and again in the open-air markets, vegetable stalls, and shops that specialize in the sale of fruits and vegetables. While others in the group were browsing through shops, caressing leather goods and shoes, inspecting jewelry and the like, I was squeezing artichokes and fondling eggplants, discussing the merits of different types of radicchio, poking through woodsy-smelling mushrooms . . . this is the way I like to shop.

Italians love vegetables. From late May through mid-October the vegetables my mother served—breakfast (zucchini flowers dipped in batter and fried), lunch, and dinner—came from the huge garden some 20 yards from her kitchen table. *Fresh* was the operative word.

Still, today, because I live less than 100 yards from a very good supermarket, I shop for vegetables the day or evening I plan to use them. But I'm picky about vegetables, and I will drive 15 miles for some rapini. I know a place that always has the slim Japanese eggplants (and dandelion in the spring).

The point is that one of the great pleasures for the cook is selecting vegetables. It is the one food area where we can still view the bounty of nature in all its naked glory and so unadorned pick the best of the crop.

In this chapter I do a lot with roasting, a cooking technique that is very healthy but too often ignored. Roasting vegetables is convenient, because the vegetables need no extra stirring or tending. Roasting also develops the flavor of the vegetable without requiring excessive oils or fats. I loved my mother's eggplant parmigiana, but all of the olive oil she used to fry the eggplant stayed in the slices.

Special attention is given to fresh fennel, because I believe that this aromatic vegetable is too often overlooked. It lends itself to many preparations, but when it is used in combination with nothing more than tomatoes and herbs the flavor contrast is quite striking.

Verdure Arrostite

(Mixed Roast Vegetables)

A scintillating array of fresh vegetables is roasted and combined with beans and herbs, the whole process accomplished with just a small amount of olive oil. Don't worry too much about uniform size in the cut vegetables; a variety of textures just makes the dish more interesting. A perfect all-vegetable platter for a picnic, al fresco dining, or a buffet, the dish can be served warm, at room temperature, or slightly chilled.

1. Preheat the oven to 450°F. Spread the olive oil over a baking sheet that measures about 12″ × 18″. Put each vegetable into a specific area on the baking sheet, spreading them out as much as possible. Sprinkle on the garlic and herbs.

2. Roast the vegetables for 15 minutes. Remove the pan, but leave the oven on. Using two large serving spoons, mix and combine the vegetables thoroughly. Spread them across the pan evenly. Return the pan to the oven and roast for an additional 6 to 7 minutes. To test for doneness, taste one of the potatoes; it should be cooked through but firm and not soft. The dish can be refrigerated for up to 4 or 5 days.

Serves 4 to 6
Calories: 220 per serving

2 tablespoons extra-virgin olive oil

½ pound (about 2 small) yellow squash, cubed

½ pound (about 2 small) zucchini, cubed

1 pound (about 8 small) red-skinned potatoes, cut into small wedges

1 medium-size green bell pepper, cored, seeded, and cut into strips

1 medium-size red or yellow bell pepper, cored, seeded, and cut into strips

2 cups cooked Great Northern beans or drained and rinsed canned cannellini beans

1 28-ounce can peeled whole tomatoes, drained and crushed

2 cloves garlic, minced

2 teaspoons dried oregano, crumbled

¼ cup packed torn fresh basil leaves or 1 teaspoon dried

Salt and pepper to taste

Rapini con Fagioli

(Rapini with Beans)

Rapini, cima di rapa, broccoli rabe . . . it goes by a number of different names, but the final word is that this soft and crunchy, sweet and bitter green—turnip tops, actually—is exquisite eating just about any way it is prepared. Its wedding with garlic and olive oil is a marriage made in taste heaven, but to this bliss I add some beans, which seals the ceremony of flavor even more. (See Index for more recipes using the vegetable.) Serve this recipe as a side dish with any chicken, veal, or pork dish.

2 pounds rapini
1 cup water
2 cloves garlic, minced
3 tablespoons extra-virgin olive oil
2 cups cooked Great Northern beans or drained and rinsed canned cannellini beans
Salt and freshly ground black pepper to taste
¼ teaspoon crushed red pepper flakes (optional)

1. Cut off and discard 3 to 4 inches of the stem of the rapini; wash in a large bowl of cold water, changing the water twice, but do not shake it dry or dry it in any other way; the more water clinging to the leaves, the better. Place the rapini and water in a large pot set over medium heat. Cover the pot and cook until the rapini is tender, 6 to 7 minutes. Lift the rapini out of the pot with a fork and set aside.

2. In a large skillet over medium-high heat, sauté the garlic in the oil for 2 minutes, stirring constantly. Do not let the garlic darken too much. Add the beans and continue to cook and stir for 1 minute. Add the rapini, salt, and pepper. Cook for 2 minutes longer, stirring constantly, until the rapini is hot. Add the red pepper flakes if desired. Serve at once or at room temperature.

Serves 4 to 6
Calories: 160 per serving

Rapini

This vegetable is destined for an important future. Rapini has many names: broccoli rabe, cima di rabe, cima di rapa ("top of the turnip"). It has been seen in markets mostly from fall through spring, but lately, because of increased demand, availability seems to be widening.

The flavor of rapini is incomparable. It has a sweet yet bitter flavor that transcends escarole or arugula (and it's a lot less expensive than arugula), and its soft but crunchy texture is most appealing.

When buying, look for some small fresh yellow flowers on the top of the florets; the stalks should be dark green and rather firm. If the leaves are wilted or the florets droopy, the rapini is past its prime.

Finocchio e Pomodori

(Fennel and Tomato)

The subtle anise flavor of fresh fennel is complemented by plum tomatoes, onion, and Parmesan cheese. This is a dish that can be served hot, at room temperature, or even slightly chilled, so it's perfect for doing ahead. Also, it can be served as an antipasto or as a side dish with fish or pork.

....

10–12 ounces trimmed fresh fennel bulb

3 cups water

1 28-ounce can plum tomatoes, drained and crushed

2 cloves garlic, minced

2 tablespoons extra-virgin olive oil

2 tablespoons chopped flat-leaf parsley

3 tablespoons finely chopped red onion

1 teaspoon dried oregano, crumbled

Salt and freshly ground black pepper to taste

1 tablespoon freshly grated Parmesan cheese

1. Cut the fennel bulb lengthwise through the center and remove the small tough triangular root in each half. Slice each bulb half lengthwise into strips about ¼ inch wide.

2. Place the water in a deep skillet or sauté pan large enough to hold the tomatoes and remaining ingredients. Bring the water to a boil. Add the fennel and poach for 4 to 5 minutes, until the fennel just starts to lose its firmness. Drain the water from the pan and return the pan with the fennel to the stove.

3. Add the remaining ingredients except the salt and pepper and cheese. Over medium-high heat, cook and stir for 6 to 8 minutes or until the water from the tomatoes has evaporated. Add salt and pepper.

4. Transfer the contents of the pan to a serving dish or individual plates. Sprinkle on the Parmesan cheese.

Serves 3 to 4
Calories: 125 per serving

Finocchi Gratinati
(Baked Fresh Fennel)

It seems that this wonderful vegetable has cast a spell over my taste buds—I can't seem to get enough of it. Traditionally a *finocchi gratinati* is served with a besciamella, or white sauce, but I have eschewed that in the interest of reducing fat and calories. To increase the flavor I use chicken broth instead of water for the baking and the more assertive Romano cheese instead of Parmigiano to complement the mild flavor of the fennel. Serve the fennel as a vegetable course with any type of pork dish.

....

1. Preheat the oven to 350°F. Remove the small triangular core at the base of each of the fennel halves and place the fennel in a bowl of cold water.

2. Bring a large pot of water to a boil and add the fennel and garlic. Boil for 8 to 10 minutes or until the fennel is tender when pierced with the tip of a knife. Drain the fennel and pat dry. Discard the garlic.

3. Put the chicken stock in an ovenproof ceramic or glass baking dish that is large enough to hold the fennel in one layer. Add the blanched fennel, cut side up, to the dish.

4. Combine the cheese and bread crumbs and sprinkle evenly over the fennel. Bake the fennel until the tops are golden brown. Serve at once.

4 medium-size (4- to 5-ounce) fennel bulbs, trimmed and halved lengthwise
2 cloves garlic, peeled
½ cup Chicken Stock (see Index) or lower-salt canned chicken broth
½ cup freshly grated Romano cheese
½ cup fresh bread crumbs

Serves 4
Calories: 78 per serving

Spinaci e Pomodori con Pignoli

(Spinach and Tomatoes with Pine Nuts)

The delicate texture of the spinach and tomatoes is given a bit of crunch with the addition of pine nuts. This dish is ideal for an antipasto table or a picnic, because it can be made ahead and refrigerated. However, it works nicely, too, as a side dish with veal or chicken.

....

2 10-ounce packages fresh
   spinach
½ cup water
1 pound (8–10) fresh plum
   tomatoes, peeled (see Index)
   and chopped coarse, or 1
   28-ounce can, drained and
   chopped coarse
2 tablespoons extra-virgin
   olive oil
¼ cup pine nuts
1 teaspoon dried oregano,
   crumbled
2 tablespoons chopped fresh
   basil or 1 teaspoon dried
Salt and freshly ground black
   pepper to taste
2 tablespoons freshly grated
   Parmesan cheese

1. Wash the spinach in a large bowl of cold water while breaking off any thick stems. Drain the spinach but do not dry. Place the spinach and the water in a large pot. Place the tomatoes on top of the spinach. Cover the pot, turn the heat to medium, and cook for 7 to 8 minutes, until the spinach is soft and wilted. Transfer the contents of the pot to a strainer or colander and let drain for a few minutes.

2. In a skillet or sauté pan set over medium heat, warm the oil for about 1 minute. Add the pine nuts and cook and stir for 1 minute. Add the spinach and tomato mixture to the pan along with the oregano and basil. Add the salt and pepper. Cook and stir for 2 to 3 minutes longer.

3. Transfer to a serving bowl and sprinkle with Parmesan cheese. Serve hot or let cool to room temperature or refrigerate overnight but return to room temperature to serve.

Serves 4
Calories: 166 per serving

Patate e Peperoni

(Peppers and Potatoes)

A wonderful dish that was often served by my mother, though she sometimes added soaked and dried cubes of day-old Italian bread and, on occasion, cannellini beans. My version allows the flavors of the potatoes and peppers to dominate. The twist to this dish is the abundant amount of freshly ground black pepper. And this is a great dish to serve at room temperature, so it can be made well in advance of serving time. Serve it as the vegetable with roast pork or chicken or on an antipasto buffet. The recipe can easily be cut in half.

....

1. Cook the unpeeled potatoes in boiling water until not quite cooked through—10 to 12 minutes. Drain and reserve. When cool enough to handle, cut the potatoes into quarters.

2. Put the peppers, onion, and oil in a large pot or sauté pan over medium-high heat. Stir to combine the peppers with the oil. Cover the pot and cook for 7 to 8 minutes, stirring occasionally, until the peppers are soft.

3. Add the potatoes to the pot with the peppers. Add the oregano and stir and cook for 3 to 4 minutes over medium heat, until the potatoes are starting to get brown and crusty. Add salt and pepper to taste. Serve hot or at room temperature.

1½ pounds (about 12 small) red-skinned potatoes
1 pound (about 2 medium-size) green bell peppers or ½ pound each red and green, cored, seeded, and cut into ½-inch-wide strips
½ cup chopped red onion
2 tablespoons extra-virgin olive oil
1 teaspoon dried oregano, crumbled
Salt and freshly ground black pepper to taste

Serves 6 to 8
Calories: 116 per serving

Carciofi Ripieni

(Stuffed Artichokes)

The artichoke is the quintessential Italian vegetable, its versatility outdone only by its wonderful flavor. The small, tender artichokes available in Italy are often simply sliced and sautéed, but this more elaborate preparation takes advantage of the larger globe artichoke. Buy only artichokes that are firm and have leaves that are unspotted. Serve as a first course before a roast.

1 cup fresh bread crumbs
½ cup freshly grated Romano cheese, plus additional for serving (optional)
2 teaspoons finely chopped garlic
2 tablespoons virgin olive oil
1 teaspoon balsamic vinegar or white wine vinegar
1 teaspoon dried mint, crumbled, or 1 tablespoon finely chopped fresh
Salt and freshly ground black pepper to taste
4 6- to 8-ounce artichokes
Fresh lemon juice

1. In a small bowl, mix the bread crumbs, cheese, garlic, oil, vinegar, and mint until well combined. Season with salt and pepper and set aside.

2. Cut the bases of artichokes flush and flat so they can stand upright. Bend and snap off the smaller bottom leaves. Slice about 1 inch off the top of each artichoke. Trim about ¼ inch off the points of the leaves. Wash artichokes under cold water, separating leaves slightly. Using a small pointed spoon, scrape out the fuzzy choke inside the artichoke, but be careful not to remove any of the heart.

3. Stuff the filling into the center of each artichoke and between the leaves.

4. Place the artichokes upright in a deep pot just large enough to hold them and add water to cover almost three-quarters of the artichokes. Sprinkle with the lemon juice. Bring the water to a boil, cover the pot, and lower the heat to simmer the artichokes for about 30 minutes or until the base of the artichoke is tender when pierced with the tip of a knife. Serve hot, the tops sprinkled with additional cheese if desired.

Serves 4
Calories: 169 per serving

VEGETABLES

84

Carciofi e Fagioli

(Artichokes and Beans)

Using frozen artichoke hearts makes this delicious vegetable dish come together in a matter of minutes. It can be served at room temperature or slightly chilled. Either way, serve it as a side dish with veal cutlets, any roasted meat, or roasted fowl.

....

1. In a sauté pan set over medium-high heat, warm 2 tablespoons of the oil for 1 minute. Add the artichoke hearts, parsley, and scallion and sauté gently for 3 minutes. Add the vinegar and cook for 1 minute more or until you can no longer smell the vinegar.

2. Transfer the artichokes to a serving platter and add the beans. Dress with the remaining tablespoon of oil. Season with salt and pepper and toss gently to combine. Sprinkle on the Parmesan cheese.

Serves 4
Calories: 175 per serving

3 tablespoons virgin olive oil
1 9-ounce package frozen artichoke hearts, thawed or steamed according to package directions
2 tablespoons chopped flat-leaf parsley
¼ cup chopped scallion
2 tablespoons balsamic vinegar
1 cup drained canned Great Northern beans, rinsed and patted dry
Salt and freshly ground black pepper to taste
2 tablespoons freshly grated Parmesan cheese

Bietole e Patate

(Swiss Chard and Potatoes)

This is an adaptation of a dish that my mother made in the spring, when dandelions were something of a "lawn crop." The scarcity of dandelions prompted me to use the more accessible Swiss chard. This is sort of a "univegetable" dish; the potatoes are mashed into the chard. Serve it with a roast loin of pork or veal or roast chicken.

3 pounds Swiss chard
1 pound (about 8 small) red-skinned potatoes
2 cloves garlic, sliced thin
3 tablespoons virgin olive oil
¼ cup chopped yellow onion
Salt and freshly ground black pepper to taste

1. In a large pot, steam or boil the Swiss chard until tender, 2 to 3 minutes. Remove and set aside. In the same pot, boil the potatoes until quite tender, 10 to 12 minutes. Peel the potatoes and cut them into ½-inch cubes when cool enough to handle. Set aside.

2. In a large skillet over medium heat, brown the garlic in 1 tablespoon of the oil. Discard the garlic. Add the onion and cook until softened.

3. Add the remaining oil, chard, and potatoes to the skillet with the onion. Keeping the heat on medium and using the back of a spoon or a potato masher, mash the potatoes lightly and blend them into the Swiss chard. Season with salt and pepper and serve hot.

Serves 4 to 6
Calories: 162 per serving

The best-tasting seafood is simply prepared. None of the recipes call for deep-frying or sautéing the seafood, nor do they use butter or cream. Consider the delicious alternatives for cooking seafood, which include broiling, baking, roasting, steaming, and grilling. Then enhance the flavor of the dish with herbs, quality olive oil, and vegetables as much as possible. All of these cooking methods help to keep the calorie count down and the flavor level up.

Seafood and pasta are a classic Italian combination. See the "Pasta" chapter for more recipes using fish and shellfish.

Merluzzo al Forno

(Baked Cod)

When I was young, the signal that Lent was about to begin was the smell of baccalà—dried salt cod—hitting me in the nose when I opened the door to the back porch on our house. The long fillets of cod were at their aromatic peak in their dried state, but within days my mother had tamed the strong aroma by soaking them in several changes of water. Through the Lenten season she used the baccalà in any number of dishes—with spinach or bread crumbs or with olive oil as a sauce for pasta. But the best dish used a tomato sauce, and this recipe is somewhat close to my mother's. However, I used cod fillets in place of the dried cod, since the soaking process is quite laborious and time-consuming. I like to serve this dish with polenta (see Index) and sautéed zucchini.

2 tablespoons virgin olive oil
1 tablespoon finely chopped garlic
½ cup finely chopped yellow onion
¼ cup chopped flat-leaf parsley
1 28-ounce can plum tomatoes, with juice
¼ cup chopped fresh basil or 1 teaspoon dried
1 teaspoon dried oregano, crumbled
½ teaspoon dried thyme, crumbled
4–5 grinds of black pepper
4 5- to 6-ounce cod fillets, ¾–1 inch thick

1. In a large nonreactive bowl, combine all the ingredients except the fish. Leave at room temperature for 35 to 45 minutes to blend the flavors.

2. Preheat the oven to 375°F. Place the fish in a single layer in a glass or porcelain baking dish. Pour the sauce over the fish. Bake for 20 to 25 minutes or until the fish flakes gently when tested with a fork.

3. To serve, place the fillets on individual serving plates. Using a slotted spoon, place some of the sauce over each fillet. Serve at once.

Serves 4
Calories: 243 per serving

Persico al Pomodoro e Finocchio

(*Orange Roughy with Fennel and Tomato Sauce*)

The humble and often misused orange roughy is given an aromatic sauce that cloaks it with distinction. Orange roughy is not native to the waters of Italy; there a similar dish might be made with sea bream, John Dory, or other mild white-fleshed fish.

....

1. Make the sauce. Put the onion, fennel, garlic, tomatoes, and lemon juice in a food processor fitted with the steel blade. Process with short pulses until the mixture forms a coarse puree. Transfer the sauce to a mixing bowl and season with salt and pepper.

2. In a saucepan set over medium heat, bring the sauce to a gentle boil; turn the heat to low and simmer for 8 to 10 minutes to reduce slightly. Keep the sauce warm while the fish is being cooked.

3. Preheat the broiler to its highest setting. Brush the fillets generously on both sides with the olive oil. Place the fillets on the broiler pan and set the pan under the broiler with the oven rack as close to the heat as possible.

4. Broil the fish until it is cooked through. Thin fillets will cook in a couple of minutes without turning. Thicker fillets should take no longer than 5 minutes.

5. Lay each fillet on a warm plate and spoon some sauce over it. Serve at once.

¼ cup chopped yellow onion
½ cup chopped trimmed fresh
  fennel bulb
1 small clove garlic, crushed
1 28-ounce can plum
  tomatoes, drained
1 teaspoon fresh lemon juice
Salt and freshly ground black
  pepper to taste
2 tablespoons virgin olive oil
4 6- to 8-ounce orange roughy
  fillets

Serves 4
Calories: 357 per serving

Halibut al Vapore con Finocchio

(Steamed Halibut with Fennel)

There is no vegetable that enhances fish more graciously or more flavorfully than fresh fennel. I recall eating a dish similar to this in Italy a number of years ago, but in that instance the whole fish was wrapped in fennel twigs and enclosed in a fish grill. For ease of cooking, but with a flavor that is still more pervasive, the fish is cooked *al cartoccio*—the packets or small parcels formed using aluminum foil. Roasted potatoes and grilled fresh asparagus would make nice accompaniments to the fish.

....

4 teaspoons virgin olive oil
2 medium-size (4- to 5-ounce) fresh fennel bulbs, including feathery green leaves
4 7- to 8-ounce halibut fillets, skinned
2 cloves garlic, minced
4 slices lemon

1. To prepare the packets for the fish, cut four 12-inch squares of heavy-duty aluminum foil. Brush or rub one side of each piece with 1 teaspoon of olive oil. Light a charcoal grill.

2. Wash the fennel under cold running water. Trim off any part of the bulb or the green spray that is discolored. Cut the bulb part in half lengthwise, cut out the triangular core, and cut each half lengthwise into ¼-inch strips. Coarsely chop the feathery green leaves.

3. Divide the fennel strips and leaves among the four pieces of foil, making a bed for each piece of fish. Place the fish on the fennel. Sprinkle some garlic over each fillet. Lay a lemon slice on each fillet.

4. Roll the foil loosely around the fish, crimping the edges to retain the steam. There should be an air pocket of about 2 inches between the fish and the top of the crimped foil.

5. When the coals in the grill are ash-covered, place the foil packets on the grill and cook for about 15 minutes. Test the fish for doneness by removing one of the packets from

the grill and opening it. The fish should be somewhat firm and cooked through. The best way to test it is to insert the tip of a knife into the fillet.

6. Remove the packets from the grill and transfer the fillets to warm plates. Top with some of the cooking juices from the foil. Serve at once.

Serves 4
Calories: 288 per serving

Pagello al Forno

(Baked Red Snapper)

I could have named this dish *Pagello al Mediterraneo*, since the flavors of Mediterranean cooking—capers, olives, basil, garlic—are deeply imbued in this tasty yet easy fish dish. This is a bake/poach method of cooking fish that saves time but keeps the flavor intact. Serve the fish with roasted potatoes or rice and steamed escarole or spinach or green beans.

....

4 8-ounce red snapper fillets with skin
Juice of ½ lemon
½ cup dry white wine or water
6 plum tomatoes, peeled, seeded, and chopped
½ tablespoon drained capers, rinsed
6 pitted black olives, sliced into rings
1 tablespoon extra-virgin olive oil
3–4 fresh basil leaves or ½ teaspoon dried, crumbled
2 tablespoons chopped flat-leaf parsley
1 teaspoon dried thyme, crumbled
1 clove garlic, finely chopped
Lemon wedges for garnish

1. Preheat the oven to 450°F. Place the fish fillets, skin side down, in one layer in a shallow baking pan or casserole. Pour the lemon juice and wine over the fish and let sit for 5 minutes.

2. Distribute the remaining ingredients except the lemon wedges evenly over the fish, cover the baking pan loosely with aluminum foil, and bake, covered, for 10 minutes (about 12 minutes per inch of thickness).

3. Remove the foil, place the fillets on individual serving plates, and spoon an equal amount of the pan ingredients over each. Garnish with lemon wedges.

Serves 4
Calories: 303 per serving

Scampi con Aglio e Olio e Orzo

(Shrimp with Oil and Garlic and Orzo)

One of my favorite pasta dishes is *spaghetti aglio e olio*. Here I apply the same idea to shrimp. Orzo, a small rice-shaped pasta that is most compatible with seafood, especially shrimp, stands in for the spaghetti.

....

1. Bring the water to a boil in a large pot and add salt. Cook the pasta until al dente, about 8 to 10 minutes, drain, and reserve.

2. Warm the oil in a large skillet over medium heat. When the oil is hot (but not smoking), add the garlic and sauté for 2 minutes; do not burn the garlic. Add the shrimp and move them around in the pan with a wooden spoon to coat with the oil. Cook, stirring occasionally, until the shrimp turns pink, about 5 minutes.

3. Working quickly, turn the heat to medium-low and add the reserved pasta to the skillet. Stir well to coat the pasta with the sauce. Off the heat, scoop out portions of pasta and shrimp and arrange them on individual serving plates. Shower some parsley over each plate and garnish with lemon. Serve at once.

2 quarts water
Salt to taste
½ pound orzo
½ cup extra-virgin olive oil
6 cloves garlic, peeled and
  sliced superthin lengthwise
1½–2 pounds large (about
  15–20 per pound) shrimp
Chopped flat-leaf parsley and
  fresh lemon wedges for
  garnish

Serves 6
Calories: 419 per serving

Pesce Spada al Passato
di Peperoni Arrostiti

(Swordfish with Red Pepper Sauce)

One of the best ways to cook this firm-textured, full-flavored popular Italian fish is grilling. The marinade gives it a flavorful start, and the smoky, coarse-textured sauce adds taste to an otherwise mild fish. The pepper sauce can be made a day ahead, refrigerated, and heated just before using. You can also prepare this dish with tuna or cod.

RED PEPPER SAUCE
8 pieces jarred roasted red
    bell peppers, patted dry
    with paper towels
1 tablespoon virgin olive oil
1/3 cup Chicken Stock (see
    Index) or lower-salt canned
    chicken broth
Salt and freshly ground black
    pepper to taste

MARINADE
2 sprigs fresh rosemary,
    crushed
2 cloves garlic, minced
1/3 cup virgin olive oil
2 tablespoons fresh lemon
    juice
1/2 teaspoon salt
1/2 teaspoon freshly ground
    black pepper

4 1-inch-thick 6-ounce
    swordfish steaks

1. Put all the sauce ingredients in the bowl of a food processor fitted with the steel blade or a blender and process to a smooth puree. Before using the sauce, simmer it over low heat for 3 to 4 minutes to reduce and blend the flavors.

2. Mix and combine all the ingredients for the marinade in a glass or nonreactive baking dish. Put the fish fillets in the dish and turn twice to coat. Refrigerate, covered, for at least 2 hours but no more than 8 hours.

3. Light a charcoal grill. When the coals are ash-covered, remove the fish from the marinade and pat dry. Place the fish on an oiled grill rack or fish grill. Grill the fish, turning once, until just cooked through—8 to 10 minutes, depending on the heat of the grill.

4. Place an equal amount of warm red pepper sauce on each of the serving plates. Place the swordfish fillets on the sauce. Serve at once.

Serves 4
Calories: 305 per serving

SEAFOOD

Tonno Grigliato col Contorno di Pomodoro

(Grilled Tuna with Tomato Relish)

The best way to approach this delicious fish dish is to split the work into three parts: marinate the fish, start the charcoal fire, then make the aromatic tomato relish while the coals are heating. Swordfish makes a perfect substitute for the tuna should you prefer.

1. In a glass baking dish large enough to hold the fish in one layer, combine and mix thoroughly all the marinade ingredients. Add the tuna and turn the fish four times to coat well. Marinate at room temperature, but away from excessive heat, for 30 to 40 minutes. If you wish to hold the fish longer (up to 2 hours), put it in the refrigerator.

2. Light a charcoal grill, and while the coals are heating, combine all the relish ingredients in a bowl. Stir thoroughly. Set aside for 15 to 20 minutes to allow the flavors to blend.

3. When the coals are ash-covered, remove the tuna steaks from the marinade and place them on the grill (lightly brushing the grates with oil will prevent the fish from sticking). Cook for about 5 minutes per side. It is better to undercook the tuna, so watch the heat and the cooking time.

4. To serve, put the tuna steaks on warmed plates and top each one with tomato relish.

Serves 4
Calories: 313 per serving

MARINADE
½ cup balsamic vinegar
2 tablespoons extra-virgin olive oil
2 tablespoons fresh lemon juice
1 clove garlic, minced
½ teaspoon freshly ground black pepper

4 6- to 8-ounce tuna steaks, cut about 1 inch thick

TOMATO RELISH
1½ cups diced ripe tomatoes
1 tablespoon extra-virgin olive oil
2 teaspoons minced garlic
2 tablespoons minced flat-leaf parsley
1 tablespoon drained capers, rinsed

Tonno con Salsa Salmoriglio

(Tuna with Salmoriglio Sauce)

The best method for grilling tuna is to do it the way it is done in restaurants, which is to first sear the tuna steaks, turning once, over the hottest part of the coals, then move them toward the edge of the grill to complete the cooking. Tuna cooks very quickly, so buy steaks that are at least ¾ to 1 inch thick to avoid the possibility of overcooking. In fact, it is best to undercook the tuna slightly, as it will continue to cook a bit even after it is off the heat.

A sauce of many uses, salmoriglio is important to cooks in southern Italy and Sicily. I use it here as a topping for the tuna, but I have also served salmoriglio over grilled vegetables such as asparagus or radicchio and cold as a salad dressing as well.

....

MARINADE
¼ cup olive oil
juice of one lemon
¼ teaspoon salt

4 6- to 7-ounce tuna steaks,
    ¾–1 inch thick

SALMORIGLIO SAUCE
½ cup water
⅛ teaspoon coarse or sea salt
¾ cup extra-virgin olive oil
2 cloves garlic, sliced thin
¼ cup fresh lemon juice
2 tablespoons chopped flat-
    leaf parsley
1 teaspoon dried oregano,
    crumbled

1. Marinate the fish. In a small mixing bowl, combine the oil, lemon juice, and salt. Place the tuna steaks in a single layer in a glass or nonreactive metal dish. Pour the marinade over the fish, turn once to coat fish, and place dish, covered, in the refrigerator for at least 1 hour and up to 3 hours.

2. Make the sauce. In a small saucepan over medium-high heat, heat the water and take it off the heat just before it comes to a boil. Dissolve the salt in the water at once.

3. Put the olive oil in a small bowl. Beat in the water. Add the garlic, lemon juice, parsley, and oregano and beat well until thoroughly combined.

4. Place the bowl with the sauce over a saucepan of simmering water (do not let the bottom of the bowl touch the water). Cook and stir the sauce for 4 minutes. Hold the sauce over low heat while grilling the fish.

5. Prepare the charcoal fire to grill the tuna. Lightly saturate paper towels with vegetable oil and oil the grill rack. When the coals are covered with ash, place the tuna steaks in the center part of the grill. Grill the steaks, turning once, for 3 to 4 minutes on each side (depending on the thickness of the tuna) until barely cooked through (there should be a very narrow pinkish band through the very center).

6. To serve, place each steak on a dinner plate and top with a small amount of the salmoriglio sauce.

Serves 4
Calories: 660 per serving

Cioppino

(Fish Stew)

Cioppino is to Italian-Americans what bouillabaisse is to the French. A full-flavored seafood stew that originated in San Francisco, cioppino is actually neither difficult nor time-consuming to make once you've assembled the ingredients. Make sure you use a large pot—I use a heavy 8-quart dutch oven. Serve with crusty fresh Italian bread, which is great for dipping in the sauce.

....

½ cup virgin olive oil
1 large yellow onion, chopped
1 large green bell pepper, cored, seeded, and chopped
3 ribs celery, trimmed and chopped
2 cloves garlic, crushed
½ cup chopped flat-leaf parsley
1 cup dry white wine
1 6-ounce can tomato paste
1 28-ounce can tomato puree
1 28-ounce can plum tomatoes, crushed, with juice
1 teaspoon sugar
1 large bay leaf
1 teaspoon dried basil, crumbled
1 teaspoon dried thyme, crumbled
1 tablespoon dried oregano, crumbled
1½ pounds medium-size shrimp, shelled and deveined
24 cherrystone clams, well scrubbed

1½ pounds fish fillets—firm fish such as grouper, halibut, snapper, or monkfish—cut into uniform 1-inch-square pieces
Salt and pepper to taste
Coarsely chopped parsley for garnish

1. Warm olive oil in a pot over medium-high heat. Add onion, bell pepper, celery, garlic, and parsley. Simmer and stir for 2 to 3 minutes, until onion softens. Turn heat up a bit, add wine, and simmer vigorously until the alcohol cooks off, about 3 to 4 minutes.

2. Add remaining ingredients except the seafood, salt and pepper, and garnish. Reduce heat and simmer, uncovered, for 45 minutes, stirring frequently. Maintaining a steady simmer, add the shrimp and clams and cook until the clams open (discard any clams that don't open)—about 6 minutes. Add the fish and cook for 5 to 6 minutes more, until just cooked through. Season with salt and pepper.

3. Ladle the stew into individual serving bowls and garnish with parsley.

Serves 6
Calories: 540 per serving

Fowl by itself is a lonely dish, so in each of the recipes in this chapter I have coupled the chicken or turkey with something else—tomatoes, peppers, garlic, mushrooms, spinach, herbs—to maximize the flavor. To keep the fat and cholesterol counts down, I suggest braising, roasting, broiling, grilling . . . any cooking method except frying (Italians very seldom fry fowl).

Then there is the simplicity of each of the dishes; even the fragrant and lively Chicken with Herbs and Potatoes takes only 45 minutes to make; the Breast of Chicken in Mushroom Sauce takes even less time.

In the small town where I was reared, the volunteer fire department raised money twice a year by holding what was called a "spaghetti supper." That simple name belied the fabulous feast that attracted people from miles around.

In the kitchen at the rear of the firehouse the women cooked (the men waited on tables)—and cooked and cooked: huge pots of tomato sauce simmering on the stove, pans filled with meatballs, stuffed peppers, and braciole ready to go into the ovens.

The big hit of these suppers, though, was the combination of chicken and spaghetti. There were many reasons for this, of course—portion size being one. But then there was the quality and inestimable flavor of the red sauce (made from canned homemade tomato puree), the fact that the spaghetti was always perfectly al dente, and just as important, that the chicken had been freshly killed and dressed that morning.

FOWL

The moral is that for the chicken dishes in this chapter you should buy the freshest chicken you can find, and you will enjoy the dishes that much more. And if you want to duplicate the spaghetti and chicken from those spaghetti suppers, cook some spaghetti and pile the Chicken in the Style of Rome from this chapter on top.

Pollo Vesuvio

(Chicken with Herbs and Potatoes)

Chicken Vesuvio is an extremely popular entree in Chicago's Italian restaurants. Many contend, in fact, that the dish originated in Chicago. It is simple to prepare yet deeply satisfying. The cooking starts off in a large frying pan on top of the stove and is finished in a roasting pan or casserole in the oven. Total cooking time is about 45 minutes.

1. Preheat oven to 450°F. Heat 3 tablespoons of oil in a large skillet over medium-high heat. Add half the chicken pieces, skin side down, and cook until slightly brown—about 5 minutes. Transfer chicken to a large roasting pan. Brown remaining chicken, adding 1 more tablespoon oil, if necessary, and transfer them to roasting pan.

2. Drain off all the liquid in the pan. Heat the remaining 2 tablespoons of oil in the pan over medium-high heat, add the potato wedges in a single layer, and fry, turning once or twice, until the outside begins to crisp and turn a light brown—about 4 minutes. Transfer potatoes to the pan with the chicken.

3. Sprinkle the garlic, oregano, rosemary, and parsley evenly over the chicken and potatoes. Add the pepper. Drizzle with wine.

4. Bake for 30 to 35 minutes, turning the chicken and potatoes twice, until the juice runs clear when a chicken thigh is pierced with a knife. About 5 minutes before the chicken is done, add the peas to the pan if desired. Arrange the chicken pieces and the potato wedges on a platter. Serve at once.

5–6 tablespoons virgin olive oil

1 3½- to 4-pound frying chicken, cut into 8–12 pieces

4 (about 1 pound) medium-size Idaho baking potatoes, each quartered lengthwise

4 cloves garlic, minced

2 teaspoons dried oregano, crumbled

1 teaspoon dried rosemary, crumbled

2 tablespoons minced flat-leaf parsley

Freshly ground black pepper to taste

½ cup dry white wine

1 cup frozen peas, soaked in hot water for 10 minutes (optional)

Serves 4 to 6
Calories: 500 per serving

FOWL

Pollo Brasato al Pomodoro

(Braised Chicken with Tomatoes)

The subtle flavor interplay of rosemary, garlic, and balsamic vinegar impart a wonderful fragrance to this dish. And when the tomatoes enter the picture, the taste and color palette is complete. Serve with rice and spinach sautéed in garlic and olive oil to round out the meal.

....

1 4-pound chicken, cut into
  8–12 pieces
Freshly ground black pepper
  to taste
3 tablespoons virgin olive oil
3 cloves garlic, minced
½ cup dry white wine
¼ cup balsamic vinegar
5 plum tomatoes, seeded and
  chopped coarse
½ cup sliced black olives
1 tablespoon dried rosemary,
  crumbled

1. Grind some pepper over the chicken. In a large skillet over medium-high heat, warm the olive oil for 1 minute. Add the chicken and sear on all sides, turning occasionally, for about 10 minutes. Transfer the chicken to a platter; cover with aluminum foil to keep it warm. Drain off all but about 3 tablespoons of the pan drippings.

2. Over medium heat, sauté the garlic in the pan drippings for about 1 minute. Turn up the heat to medium-high, add the wine, and simmer vigorously until the wine has reduced by half.

3. Add the vinegar, chopped tomatoes, olives, and rosemary. Return the chicken to the pan, cover, and simmer gently for 10 to 12 minutes or until the juices run clear when a chicken thigh is pierced with the tip of a paring knife. Serve immediately.

Serves 4 to 6
Calories: 464 per serving

Pollo alla Romana

(Chicken in the Style of Rome)

This chicken dish is a standard in restaurants in Rome, particularly in the summer, when it is served barely warm instead of hot from the pan. To add visual interest, use a yellow or red pepper in place of a green one.

....

1. Heat half the oil in a large skillet over medium heat for 1 minute. Add the green peppers, cover the pan, and sauté the peppers, stirring once or twice, until they soften— about 4 minutes. Transfer the peppers to a plate and reserve.

2. Add the remaining 2 tablespoons oil to the pan and sauté the garlic over medium heat for 1 minute. Add the chicken and sauté, turning once, until golden brown, about 10 minutes.

3. Increase the heat to high; add the wine and cook, shaking the pan, until the alcohol evaporates—about 1 minute. Crush the tomatoes in the cans with your hand and add them to the pan along with the oregano. Reduce the heat to medium-low; simmer, covered, over low heat for 15 minutes.

4. Add the reserved peppers to the pan and simmer, covered, for 5 minutes longer, until the chicken is cooked through. Season with salt and pepper. Cool slightly before serving.

¼ cup virgin olive oil
2 large 7- to 8-ounce green
  bell peppers, cored, seeded,
  and cut into strips about ⅛
  inch wide
1 large clove garlic, minced
1 3½- to 4-pound chicken,
  cut into 8–12 pieces
¼ cup dry white wine
2 28-ounce cans plum
  tomatoes, 1 drained
1 tablespoon dried oregano,
  crumbled
Salt and freshly ground black
  pepper to taste

Serves 4 to 6
Calories: 567 per serving

Petti di Pollo con Salsa di Funghi

(Breast of Chicken in Mushroom Sauce)

Mild-tasting domestic mushrooms are enhanced by the stronger, woodsier flavor of dried porcini. A little chicken broth and some fresh tomatoes are all that is needed to create a fresh-tasting sauce that enhances the delicate flavor of the chicken.

....

¼ ounce dried porcini or cèpes

¼ cup virgin olive oil

2 tablespoons unsalted butter

¼ cup chopped yellow onion

¼ pound fresh mushrooms, cleaned and sliced (about ½ cup)

⅓ cup dry white wine

½ pound (4–5) plum tomatoes, peeled, seeded, and chopped (see Index)

Salt and freshly ground black pepper to taste

4 (about 1½ pounds) skinless, boneless chicken breast halves

½ cup Chicken Stock (see Index) or lower-salt canned chicken broth

1. Soak the dried porcini in warm water for 10 minutes.

2. In a small skillet over medium heat, heat half the oil and half the butter. Add the onion and sliced mushrooms and sauté for about 2 minutes, until the onions soften and the mushrooms give off their moisture. Add the wine and cook until the alcohol evaporates—about 1 minute. Add the tomatoes and crush them with the back of a large spoon. Add the reserved porcini, including the strained soaking liquid. Simmer the sauce over medium-high heat to reduce slightly—about 3 minutes. Season with salt and pepper.

3. Meanwhile, in a large skillet over medium-high heat, cook the chicken breasts in the remaining oil and butter for 5 minutes, turning once, until nicely browned on both sides. Drain off excess pan drippings. Add the stock and cook for 2 to 3 minutes longer or until the breasts are cooked through.

4. Add the mushroom sauce to the chicken. Stir well and cook for 1 minute. Serve at once.

Serves 4
Calories: 360 per serving

Pollo all Diavolo

(Spicy Broiled Chicken)

Diavolo means "devilish" or "wicked" implying "hot," and there is some of both in this dish. The spiciness can be controlled by varying the amount of crushed red pepper flakes. The chicken can be grilled over charcoal if desired. Serve the chicken with *Rapini con Fagioli* or *Patate e Peperoni* (see Index).

....

1. Combine the olive oil, red pepper flakes, and rosemary in a small bowl. Set aside to blend the flavors for up to 1 hour.

2. Preheat the broiler. Brush both sides of the chicken lavishly with the pepper-infused oil and broil about 5 inches from the heat for about 15 minutes on each side or until cooked through. If you would like the chicken to be hotter, brush it once or twice with the oil while it is cooking. Sprinkle with parsley just before serving.

¼ cup extra-virgin olive oil
½ teaspoon crushed red pepper flakes
1 teaspoon dried rosemary, crumbled
1 2½- to 3-pound broiling chicken, quartered
Chopped flat-leaf parsley for garnish

Serves 2 to 4
Calories: 389 per serving

Pollo con Spinaci e Fagioli

(Chicken with Spinach and Beans)

The beans become a side dish in this one-plate meal. The spinach can be prepared up to 1 hour ahead and kept at room temperature. Similarly, the bean salad can be prepared ahead. Once the chicken has been cooked, reheat the spinach and the meal is done.

....

1 10-ounce package fresh spinach, washed, coarse stems removed
1 tablespoon virgin olive oil
2 cloves garlic, minced
2 tablespoons pine nuts
Freshly ground black pepper to taste
2 10-ounce whole boneless, skinless chicken breasts, split and gently pounded to flatten
Bean Salad (recipe follows)

1. In a large skillet or pot over medium heat, cook the spinach with the water clinging to its leaves until it is wilted and soft, 4 to 5 minutes. Drain excess water.

2. Preheat the broiler. In a large skillet or sauté pan set over medium heat, warm the olive oil for 1 minute. Add the reserved spinach, garlic, and pine nuts. Cook and stir for 3 minutes to blend the flavors. Season with pepper and set aside.

3. Place the chicken breasts on a broiler pan and set the pan on an oven rack about 5 inches from the heat. Broil the breasts, turning once, until they are cooked through—3 to 4 minutes on each side.

4. Reheat the spinach if necessary. Distribute the spinach evenly among four heated serving plates. Place one chicken breast on top of the spinach. Place some of the Bean Salad on each plate. Serve at once.

1. In a small mixing bowl, combine the beans, celery, tomatoes, and red onion.

2. Whisk together the oil, vinegar, and oregano. Season with salt and pepper. Add the dressing to the bean mixture and toss gently.

Serves 4
Calories: 383 per serving

BEAN SALAD
1 15-ounce can Great
   Northern beans, drained,
   rinsed, and patted dry
½ cup chopped celery
½ cup chopped tomato
¼ cup chopped red onion
3 tablespoons extra-virgin
   olive oil
1 teaspoon balsamic vinegar
½ teaspoon dried oregano,
   crumbled
Salt and freshly ground black
   pepper to taste

Fesa di Tacchino con Salsa di Funghi

(Turkey Breasts with Mushroom Sauce)

When marinated in garlic and spices and topped with Mushroom Sauce after cooking, mild-mannered turkey breasts take on an exceptional flavor. Spinach sautéed in garlic and olive oil and roasted potatoes or rice would be the perfect accompaniments.

....

½ cup virgin olive oil

3 cloves garlic, minced

1 teaspoon dried oregano, crumbled

1 teaspoon dried thyme, crumbled

¼ cup chopped yellow onion

4 5- to 6-ounce turkey breast tenderloins, gently pounded to flatten

1 cup Mushroom Sauce (recipe follows)

1. In a shallow rectangular glass or ceramic dish, combine the oil, garlic, oregano, thyme, and onion. Place the turkey in the marinade and turn three times to coat well. Cover and chill for up to 3 hours.

2. Preheat the broiler. Remove the turkey from the marinade and place on a broiler pan. Place the pan under the preheated broiler about 5 inches from the heat. Cook the turkey, turning it once, until it is cooked through, about 2 to 3 minutes on each side, depending on thickness.

3. Transfer the turkey to individual serving plates and top with the Mushroom Sauce. Serve at once.

Serves 4

Calories: 302 per serving (without sauce)

Mushroom Sauce

This all-purpose sauce can be used on grilled chicken breasts, veal scallops, and pork cutlets or pork chops as well as the broiled turkey. Also, it can be added to a risotto. The sauce is a breeze to make and can be refrigerated for 4 days. Simmer the sauce for 5 minutes before using if it has been refrigerated.

....

Heat the oil in a heavy 2- to 3-quart pan over medium heat. Add the onion and sauté until softened, about 2 minutes. Add the garlic and cook and stir for another 2 minutes. Add the tomatoes, mushrooms, parsley, and oregano. Simmer the sauce for 45 minutes. Season with salt and pepper.

Makes about 1 quart
Calories: 33 per ¼ cup serving

2 tablespoons extra-virgin olive oil

1 small yellow onion, chopped fine

1 clove garlic, chopped fine

1 28-ounce can plum tomatoes, drained

1 pound fresh mushrooms, cleaned and sliced

1 tablespoon chopped flat-leaf parsley

1 teaspoon dried oregano, crumbled

Salt and freshly ground black pepper to taste

While meats are important in the Italian repertoire of cooking, they do offer a challenge when it comes to reducing fat and cholesterol. Indeed, it is virtually impossible to do a soffritto (a sauté of vegetables) for the *Ossobuco* without using some butter, but it is only 2 tablespoons—not enough to worry about.

However, techniques such as marinating the meat, as in Roast Pork with Fennel, combining pork chops with a zesty low-fat pizzaiola sauce, and pan-broiling steak and coupling it with tomatoes, peppers, and mushrooms keep the flavor level high and the fat level low.

In any case, it is a good idea to trim any excess fat from all cuts of meat and not to use any cream or extra butter in sauces served with meat. In fact the Tomato and Vegetable Sauce in the "Pasta" chapter (see Index) works nicely should you feel the need for a sauce with the Veal Chops or the Stuffed Pork Loin.

Ossobuco

(Braised Veal Shanks)

Ossobuco, or stewed shanks of veal, is a classic Milanese dish. A true Milanese might disagree with the use of tomatoes, but I am of the opinion that the tomatoes add necessary flavor and interest. Just as important to this dish is the gremolada, a piquant garnish that adds the perfect final touch. The classic accompaniment to ossobuco is risotto Milanese (see Index), but you could serve it with a short pasta and a fresh tomato sauce.

2 tablespoons unsalted butter

2 tablespoons virgin olive oil

1 cup finely chopped yellow onion

½ cup finely chopped carrot

½ cup finely chopped celery

1 clove garlic, chopped fine

Freshly ground black pepper to taste

4 veal shanks, 3½ inches in diameter and 1½–2 inches thick, each with string tied around the circumference

¼ cup unbleached all-purpose flour

½ cup dry white wine

1 28-ounce can plum tomatoes, with juice, tomatoes chopped coarse

1 cup Chicken Stock (see Index) or lower-salt canned chicken broth

½ teaspoon dried thyme, crumbled

½ teaspoon dried basil, crumbled

1 bay leaf

1. In a 4- to 5-quart dutch oven or heavy pot over medium heat, melt the butter and oil until they just start to bubble. Add the onion, carrot, celery, and garlic. Cook, stirring occasionally, until the vegetables soften slightly—about 10 minutes.

2. Grind black pepper on each of the veal shanks. Dredge the meat in the flour and shake off the excess. Add the meat to the pot and brown the meat, turning as needed, on all sides.

3. Turn the heat to high, add the wine, and boil rapidly for 2 to 3 minutes to cook off the alcohol. Reduce the heat to medium. Add the tomatoes, stock, and seasonings. Cover the pot and cook over low heat for 1 to 1½ hours, stirring occasionally, adding stock if necessary, until the veal is fork-tender.

4. Meanwhile, combine the ingredients for the gremolada.

5. To serve, remove the string from the veal shanks and arrange them on a heated platter. Spoon the sauce and vegetables from the pot over and around the veal. Sprinkle the veal with the gremolada. Serve at once.

Serves 4
Calories: 370 per serving

GREMOLADA
1 tablespoon grated lemon zest
1 teaspoon finely chopped garlic
1 tablespoon finely chopped flat-leaf parsley

Costolette di Vitello

(Veal Chops)

The golden color so highly prized in Milanese foods—during the Renaissance gold was believed to be good for the heart—is achievable only if these chops are pounded until flat enough for quick cooking, yet the cook must take care to preserve the meat's texture. It is this purity that makes the dish special, and many an Italian restaurant is judged by its skill in producing the dish. Still, this magnificent veal dish in the Milanese style takes less than 30 minutes from start to finish. It is a bit rich and should be considered a splurge. Serve the chops with rice or roasted potatoes and vegetables.

....

4 8- to 10-ounce veal loin
chops, 1½ to 2 inches thick
½ cup fresh bread crumbs
¼ cup freshly grated
Parmesan cheese
¼ teaspoon freshly ground
black pepper
2 large eggs
2 tablespoons unsalted butter
2 tablespoons virgin olive oil
Lemon wedges for garnish

1. Place a veal chop between two sheets of wax paper and using a meat pounder pound firmly, working from around the bone toward the edge until the meat is less than ¼ inch thick. Pound the remaining chops in the same way.

2. In a mixing bowl, combine the bread crumbs, cheese, and pepper. Spread the mixture on a large plate or a sheet of aluminum foil. In a bowl or on a plate large enough to hold one of the flattened chops, beat the eggs lightly. Dip each chop in the egg, lightly coating both sides, then in the bread crumbs on both sides. Firmly press the bread crumbs into the chops with the palm of your hand. Put the chops on a plate and refrigerate for at least 30 minutes, up to 1 hour.

3. Preheat the oven to 350°F. In a large nonstick skillet or sauté pan (the chops will be quite large, so they probably will not all fit into the pan at once) over medium-high heat, heat the butter and oil until it just starts to foam lightly. Sauté one or two chops at a time

for 4 to 5 minutes on each side, until cooked through and the crust is golden brown. As the chops are cooked, transfer them to a heatproof plate and keep warm in the oven. Serve with lemon wedges.

Serves 4
Calories: 361 per serving

Scaloppine al Marsala

(Veal Scallops with Marsala)

A simple and easy veal dish that, before my high-cholesterol days, I served with a luscious fettuccine Alfredo. These days I serve the veal with sautéed fresh spinach and roasted potatoes, a combination that actually is more pleasing than the pasta.

....

4 5- to 6-ounce veal scallops
½ cup unbleached all-purpose
  flour
⅛ teaspoon freshly ground
  black pepper
4 tablespoons unsalted butter
3 tablespoons virgin olive oil
1 cup dry marsala
2 tablespoons fresh lemon
  juice

1. Pound the veal between sheets of wax paper to a thickness of ¼ inch or slightly less. Set aside. On a sheet of aluminum foil, combine the flour and pepper.

2. In a large nonstick skillet or sauté pan set over medium-high heat, melt 2 tablespoons of the butter and oil. Just as the butter starts to foam, dredge each scallop in the flour, shaking off the excess, and cook the veal for 2 minutes on each side, until cooked through and golden brown. Place the veal on a warm platter. Pour off most of the fat from the sauté pan.

3. Add the marsala, turn up the heat, and boil briskly for 2 to 3 minutes, until the alcohol has evaporated and the liquid has reduced by half, all the while scraping the bottom of the pan with a spatula. Swirl in the remaining 2 tablespoons butter and the lemon juice and cook for 1 minute more.

4. Spoon the sauce over the veal and serve at once.

Serves 4
Calories: 417 per serving

Medaglioni di Vitello alla Griglia con Peperoni e Cipolle

(Grilled Medallions of Veal with Onions and Peppers)

The important thing to know about this dish is that the veal should not be overcooked. Note, too, that the veal is brushed with the marinade rather than steeping in it; otherwise the delicate flavor of the veal will become secondary, and that would be a waste. If you would prefer not to grill the veal, then sauté it in a small amount of olive oil until just medium-rare. This recipe is an adaptation of a dish that I was served in a restaurant in Chicago and fell in love with.

1. In a bowl, combine half the thyme, oregano, garlic, and oil and let sit for about 30 minutes. Brush both sides of the veal with this mixture and put veal in the refrigerator for at least 1 hour and up to 3 hours.

2. In a large skillet or sauté pan, warm the remaining olive oil over medium-high heat. Add the peppers and onions and cook and stir for 3 minutes; do not let the onions brown. Add the tomatoes and the remaining garlic, thyme, and oregano. Simmer the sauce for 15 minutes. Reduce the heat to low, cover the pan, and cook for 10 minutes longer. The sauce should be rather thick and not runny; if it appears too watery, uncover the pan, turn up the heat, and cook vigorously to evaporate any excess moisture. Set the sauce aside while you prepare a charcoal grill.

3. When the coals are gray, grill veal until medium-rare, about 2 minutes on each side. Reheat sauce, place some of it on each plate, and top with two of the veal medallions.

2 tablespoons dried thyme, crumbled

2 tablespoons dried oregano, crumbled

4 cloves garlic, peeled

¼ cup virgin olive oil

8 3-ounce veal medallions

1 green bell pepper, cored, seeded, and julienned

1 red bell pepper, cored, seeded, and julienned

1 medium-size yellow onion, chopped

1 28-ounce can plum tomatoes, drained and crushed

Serves 4
Calories: 376 per serving

MEATS

Maiale Arrosto Agli Aromi

(Roast Pork with Fennel)

Marinating the pork overnight adds a great deal of flavor to this easy-to-prepare dish. Serve the roast with *Patate e Peperoni, Carciofi e Fagioli,* or *Risotto alla Milanese* (see Index).

....

1 cup Chicken Stock (see Index) or lower-salt canned chicken broth

1 cup dry white wine

1 tablespoon fennel seed

½ cup chopped yellow onion

1 tablespoon dried rosemary, crumbled

2 cloves garlic, peeled

1 bay leaf

⅛ teaspoon freshly ground black pepper

2 pounds boneless pork loin

3 tablespoons virgin olive oil

1. In a large nonreactive pan or ovenproof dish, combine everything except the pork and oil. Stir well to combine. Place the pork in the marinade and turn it several times to coat well. Marinate for at least 2 hours or overnight, turning the pork one more time several hours later.

2. The next day, remove the pork from the marinade and preheat the oven to 325°F. In a roasting pan large enough to hold the pork, warm the olive oil over medium-high heat. Add the pork to the pan and brown the roast on all sides. Off the heat, add enough of the marinade to the roasting pan to get to a depth of about ¼ inch.

3. Roast the pork for about 2 hours, basting it every 30 minutes with the marinade, adding marinade as needed. When the pork is done, let it rest for 10 minutes before slicing and serving.

Serves 4
Calories: 481 per serving

Costolette di Maiale alla Pizzaiola

(Pork Chops in Herb and Tomato Sauce)

My mother would begin a meat sauce recipe in this fashion, by cooking pork chops in tomatoes. Ultimately, though, she would fish the pork chops out of the sauce, coarsely chop the meat, and put it back into the sauce. In this recipe I choose to leave the pork chops intact and serve them draped with some of the sauce. Orzo pasta and sautééd zucchini would be a nice accompaniment to this dish.

1. Make the sauce. In a saucepan over medium heat, warm 3 tablespoons of the oil for 1 minute. Add the onion and sauté for 1 minute. Add the garlic and cook until the onions just begin to soften, 3 to 4 minutes. Add the thyme, fennel seed, tomatoes, and parsley. Season with salt and pepper. Simmer the sauce for 30 minutes.

2. In a skillet or sauté pan large enough to hold the pork chops in one layer, warm the remaining oil over medium-high heat for 1 minute. Add the pork chops and cook them for 3 to 4 minutes on each side, until they are nicely browned. Drain off any excess oil.

3. Pour the tomato sauce over the chops, cover the pan, and cook over low heat for 15 to 20 minutes or until the chops are cooked through. Serve the chops with some of the sauce spooned over the top.

5 tablespoons virgin olive oil
1 cup coarsely chopped yellow onion
1 clove garlic, minced
½ teaspoon dried thyme, crumbled
1 tablespoon fennel seed
2 cups drained and crushed canned plum tomatoes
2 tablespoons chopped flat-leaf parsley
Salt and freshly ground black pepper to taste
4 center-cut pork chops, trimmed of fat

Serves 4
Calories: 346 per serving

Involtini di Maiale

(Stuffed Pork Loin)

The word *involtini* signifies rolls of meat (or fish) that contain various stuffings. Each region of Italy sets its own direction in this regard. For example, a Neapolitan stuffing would be tomatoes and mozzarella, while a Modenese stuffing would undoubtedly include prosciutto or some type of sausage or salami. The stuffing I use here is a simple puree of fresh fennel flavored with garlic and Parmesan cheese. If you wish, thin slivers of prosciutto can be added to the fennel puree.

1 cup (about 5 ounces trimmed) chopped fresh fennel bulb
2 cloves garlic, peeled
2 tablespoons freshly grated Parmesan cheese
Salt and freshly ground black pepper to taste
2 6- to 7-ounce boneless loin pork chops, butterflied
2 teaspoons Dijon mustard
¼ cup unbleached all-purpose flour
2 tablespoons virgin olive oil
1 tablespoon unsalted butter

1. In a saucepan, blanch the fennel in boiling water until it is just barely tender. Cool slightly and place in a food processor fitted with the steel blade. Add the garlic and Parmesan cheese. Process until a smooth puree is formed—less than 1 minute. Season with salt and pepper.

2. Between sheets of wax paper, pound each of the pork chops until they are about 8 inches long by 4 to 5 inches wide. Smear 1 teaspoon of the mustard over each flattened chop. Using the back of a spoon, spread a thin layer of the fennel puree over the mustard, leaving about a ½-inch border all around (you may have some fennel puree left over; use it in a frittata or a soup). Starting from the short end of the chop, roll it tightly. Using kitchen string, tie the meat around the middle in two places (involtini can be prepared up to 2 hours ahead and held in the refrigerator at this point).

3. Flour each involtino lightly. In a skillet or sauté pan set over medium-high heat, warm the oil and butter. When the butter begins to foam, add the meat to the pan and brown the rolls on all sides, turning as needed. Reduce the heat to medium-low and cook slowly until cooked through, 7 to 8 minutes. Serve at once.

Serves 2
Calories: 567 per serving

Bistecca alla Pizzaiola con Peperoni e Funghi

(Pan-Broiled Steak with Tomatoes, Peppers, and Mushrooms)

A great way to turn an inexpensive cut of meat into a delicious main dish. Use boneless chuck and serve with roasted potatoes and fava beans or sautéed zucchini.

....

¼ cup virgin olive oil

1 green bell pepper, cored, seeded, and sliced into ¼-inch strips

½ pound fresh mushrooms, cleaned and sliced

2 cloves garlic, minced

1 28-ounce can plum tomatoes, drained and crushed

½ teaspoon dried oregano, crumbled

½ teaspoon dried basil, crumbled

⅛ teaspoon crushed red pepper flakes

Salt and freshly ground black pepper to taste

1 1¼-pound boneless chuck steak

1. In a medium-size skillet or sauté pan set over medium-high heat, heat half the olive oil for 1 minute. Add the peppers, cover the pan, and cook for 3 minutes. Add the mushrooms and garlic and cook and stir until the mushrooms begin to turn light brown, about 4 minutes. Add the tomatoes, oregano, basil, and crushed red pepper flakes. Cook over medium heat, stirring frequently, until most of the liquid from the tomatoes has evaporated, about 15 to 20 minutes. Season with salt and pepper.

2. In a large skillet or sauté pan set over medium-high heat, heat the remaining oil for 1 minute. Brown the steak on each side for 1 minute and then cook to the desired degree of doneness. Slice thin on a diagonal and top each portion with some of the sauce. Serve at once.

Serves 4
Calories: 366 per serving

I had a great time concocting these pasta recipes. Pasta and I are like peas in
a pod, and pasta with vegetables has been a passion my entire life.

The real fun came, though, in creating delicious pasta dishes that were
low in fat and cholesterol. As I started to outline some ideas for dishes, it
became apparent that my major thrust would be in pairing pasta with
vegetables. I figured that I couldn't go wrong by combining two healthy
foods. Now the challenge was to inject some flavor into this mix, so I turned
first to vegetables that would add a distinctive flavor and needed little taste
support from other ingredients. Eggplant, mushrooms, escarole, rapini, and
artichokes filled that requirement nicely. Then it was on to the additional
fillips of taste—herbs, garlic, tomatoes (fresh and sun-dried)—necessary to
round out a dish. I was a regular morning visitor to the vegetable stands
during the two weeks or so that it took me to complete the pasta with
vegetables section. It was, indeed, a section of this book that I hated to leave.

I knew it was then on to pasta with seafood, so I didn't take it too
badly. Now I had the chance to play some slightly different tunes in the pasta
songbook. Pasta with shrimp, pasta with clams, pasta with scallops . . . I was
really hitting my stride. As each recipe was tested and perfected, it was as if
I was doing these healthy and delicious recipes for myself; not as a part of a
cookbook, but for me and my family to enjoy. I was like a kid in a candy
store.

PASTA

And I didn't want to stop (enough with the pasta, already), so I rolled on into more pasta. Ravioli, flavored pasta, gnocchi—homemade pastas that are truly easy to make and will enhance any special occasion.

Finally I present some additional sauces that you can serve over the pasta of your choosing. The sauces used in the Italian cooking repertoire are really quite simple and straightforward, but Italians use sauces to do more than complement a dish—sauces often *are* the dish. For example, pasta without some kind of sauce would be boring, but the sauce plays just as important a taste role as the pasta, and very often, long after the last piece of pasta has been eaten, the sauce left in the bottom of the bowl is scooped up with chunks of bread—sort of a short meal after a long meal.

Every year, as summer drew to an end, my mother would begin the process of turning many bushels of fresh tomatoes from the garden into tomato sauce. Each day she would can 10, 15, or 20 quarts of tomatoes, until eventually the shelves in the cellar held up to 200 quarts of "red gold." She called it a sauce, but it was really a thick puree of fresh tomatoes with a few leaves of fresh basil. The real sauce started when she emptied one of those quart jars into a pot in which onion and garlic had been sautéed in olive oil. The end result was stupendous, a sauce that still makes my mouth water when I think about it.

In this last section I offer some classic sauces—pesto, marinara—and expand from there into sauces with deep Calabrian roots, Anchovy Sauce, Walnut Sauce, a sauce that I love to use on ravioli but find works just as well with other types of pasta. And though I suggest using the Squid Sauce over pasta, I have been known to serve it as is as an appetizer.

A bonus: never once in this tasty array of sauces are animal fats used.

Pasta with Vegetables

Spaghetti alle Melanzane

(Spaghetti with Eggplant)

A favorite summertime pasta dish from my mother's kitchen, made when the eggplants in her garden were at their peak flavor. If you select eggplant that is firm and slender, you won't have to go through the customary salting and pressing. The eggplant weight is approximate; a bit more or less works just fine. Peel the eggplant if the skin seems too tough. The intensity of the sauce can be increased by adding ½ teaspoon crushed red pepper flakes.

....

¾ pound eggplant, cut into ¼- to ½-inch cubes

About 2 heaped tablespoons sea salt or kosher salt

1 clove garlic, chopped fine

¼ cup chopped yellow onion

¼ cup virgin olive oil

¼ cup finely chopped flat-leaf parsley

2 28-ounce cans plum tomatoes, 1 drained

6–8 fresh basil leaves (to taste), torn, or 1 teaspoon dried, crumbled

2 teaspoons dried oregano, crumbled

1 gallon water

Salt to taste

¾ pound spaghetti

Freshly grated Parmesan cheese for serving (optional)

1. Put eggplant cubes in a large bowl and sprinkle with sea salt. Place a plate and a weight (heavy can) on top and set aside for up to 2 hours. Drain the bitter liquids from the bowl; rinse eggplant thoroughly. Pat dry.

2. In a large skillet over medium-high heat, sauté the garlic and onion in the olive oil for 2 minutes. Add the parsley and eggplant and cook and stir for 2 minutes.

3. Reduce the heat to medium-low and add the tomatoes. Cook and stir for 6 to 7 minutes, breaking up the tomatoes with a wooden spoon. Add the basil and oregano.

4. Increase the heat to medium-high and bring the sauce to a slow boil. Reduce the heat and simmer the sauce for 30 minutes or until excess water has evaporated (do not cook the sauce longer than 1 hour).

5. Bring water to boil in a large pot, add salt, and cook pasta until al dente, about 8 to 10 minutes. Drain the pasta and put it in a serving bowl. Pour the sauce over the pasta; toss gently and quickly. Serve in individual serving bowls and pass the cheese separately.

Serves 4
Calories: 546 per serving

PASTA

About Eggplant

The long, thin purple Asian eggplant is not as bitter as the more globular, Western eggplant. Either can be used for the eggplant recipes in this book, but the Western eggplant may require salting and pressing to rid it of the bitter juices that would affect the flavor of the dish.

Eggplant should be salted and pressed if when sliced it reveals a large number of seeds, especially toward the more bulbous end.

To take the bitterness out of eggplant, slice it (and peel it if the recipe so indicates) and lay the slices in layers in a colander set in the sink or in a bowl, sprinkling each layer with salt. Place some paper towels over the top layer and a plate over the paper. Set a weight (such as a heavy can) on the plate. After about 45 minutes, rinse the eggplant slices and pat dry.

When buying eggplant, look for those that have a tight nonwrinkly skin and are firm to the touch.

Fettuccine con Aglio e Olio e Escarole

(Noodles with Oil, Garlic, and Escarole)

Quick, easy, delicious, and healthy, this dish is one of my favorites, especially when I am in need of a fast pasta fix. In fact you can make the sauce while the pasta is cooking, so the total time at the stove from start to finish is about 10 minutes.

2 pounds escarole
4 quarts water
Salt to taste
¾ pound fettuccine
2 large cloves garlic, sliced
½ cup extra-virgin olive oil
¼ cup finely chopped flat-leaf
  parsley
⅛ teaspoon crushed red
  pepper flakes
Freshly ground black pepper
  to taste

1. To prepare the escarole, cut off the bottom and wash the leaves thoroughly in several changes of water. Slice the leaves lengthwise into two or three strips. Plunge the leaves into rapidly boiling water and cook for 4 minutes. Drain and set aside. When the escarole is cool enough to handle, squeeze the leaves between your hands to rid them of excess water.

2. Bring the water to a boil in a large pot, add salt, and cook the pasta until al dente, about 7 to 8 minutes.

3. While pasta is cooking, make the sauce. In a sauté pan or skillet large enough to hold all the cooked pasta, brown the garlic in the oil over medium-high heat. Don't let the garlic get too dark, or sauce will not be as fragrant. Remove garlic from pan and discard.

4. Add the parsley, red pepper flakes, and cooked escarole to the pan and stir well to coat the escarole with the oil. Reduce the heat to medium and cook and stir for 1 minute.

5. Drain the pasta well and add it to the pan with the escarole. Stir and mix with enthusiasm for 1 minute. Add salt to taste and 3 or 4 grinds of pepper. Serve at once.

Serves 4 to 6
Calories: 401 per serving

PASTA

Olive Oil

Simply put, the best olive oil to use in a salad, a pesto sauce, or a dish where the olive oil plays a predominant role is *olio d'oliva extra vergine*, or extra-virgin olive oil. From that point on it is a matter of budget and taste. The way it works is that the lower the acidity (maximum of 1 percent for extra virgin), the better the oil. Color is not a basis for determining the quality of an oil; rather it is the clean pure taste that tells the taste and quality story.

Olio d'oliva sopraffino vergine (superfine virgin olive oil) and *olio d'oliva fino vergine* (virgin olive oil) are perfectly acceptable all-purpose oils for general cooking purposes.

Ziti al Sugo di Funghi

(Ziti with Mushroom Sauce)

Once the initial prep work is done, this fragrant sauce can be made in less than 30 minutes. When cleaning fresh mushrooms, do not soak them in water: rather brush them quickly under running water with a mushroom brush or paper towel. This method helps to cut down on the water thrown off by the mushrooms during cooking. Rigatoni or fusilli can be used instead of ziti.

½ pound fresh mushrooms, cleaned and sliced lengthwise ⅛ inch thick

½ cup finely chopped yellow onion

2 tablespoons extra-virgin olive oil

2 28-ounce cans plum tomatoes, drained

1 teaspoon dried basil, crumbled

½ cup loosely packed flat-leaf parsley leaves, chopped

2 small cloves garlic, put through a press

6 quarts water

Salt to taste

¾ pound ziti

Freshly grated Parmesan cheese for serving

1. In a large sauté pan or skillet over medium-high heat, sauté the mushrooms and onion in the olive oil, stirring constantly, until the mushrooms take on some color and start to throw off water—3 to 4 minutes.

2. Reduce the heat to medium and add the tomatoes one by one, crushing each with your hand as it goes into the pan. Add the basil, parsley, and garlic.

3. Increase the heat to medium-high and keep the sauce at a steady simmer for 15 to 20 minutes, stirring frequently, until most of the water has evaporated. (Draw a wooden spoon through the sauce. If no water seeps into the path left by the spoon, the sauce is ready.)

4. While the sauce is cooking, bring the water to a boil, add salt to taste, and cook the ziti until it is al dente, about 8 to 10 minutes. Drain and place in a large serving bowl. Pour the sauce over the pasta and stir quickly and gently. Serve at once with Parmesan cheese on the side.

Serves 4 to 6
Calories: 321 per serving

Salt for Cooking Pasta

The usual amount of salt used for cooking pasta is 1½ tablespoons for 4 quarts of water, 2 tablespoons for 6 quarts of water.

Penne con Salsa Liguria

(Penne with Sauce Liguria)

Liguria is a narrow and cozy region that stretches from France and on through Genoa, winding down the coast, ending in La Spezia. The food in this region is strongly influenced by the warm Mediterranean sea and the strong sun. Fresh basil, exquisite olive oil, sun-dried tomatoes . . . there is plenty to work with. The sauce requires no cooking and works beautifully either hot or cold. Its fragrant goodness comes from giving the ingredients time to blend flavors, so make the sauce at least 1 hour before using; even 1 day ahead is fine.

¼ cup pine nuts

5 tablespoons extra-virgin olive oil

1 cup drained oil-packed sun-dried tomatoes, cut into ⅛-inch strips and patted dry

1 cup loosely packed fresh basil leaves, torn

½ cup oil-cured black olives such as Kalamata or Lugano, pitted and chopped coarse

2 cloves garlic, chopped fine

4 quarts water

Salt to taste

¾ pound penne or rigatoni

1. In a small sauté or frying pan over medium heat, toast the pine nuts in 1 tablespoon of the olive oil until just lightly browned, 2 to 3 minutes. Set aside.

2. In a mixing bowl, combine the sun-dried tomatoes, remaining olive oil, basil, olives, and garlic. Add the pine nuts and toss lightly to blend. Set the sauce aside for at least 1 hour.

3. Bring the water to a boil in a large pot, add salt, and cook the pasta according to the package directions, until al dente. Drain and put it in a large pasta serving bowl. Pour the sauce over the pasta and toss quickly to combine. Serve at once.

Serves 4 to 6
Calories: 454 per serving

Rigatoni ai Peperoni Variegati

(Rigatoni with Sweet Peppers)

The secret to the success of this flavorful pasta dish is the proper cooking of the peppers: a "slow sauté" in a covered skillet before the tomatoes are added. When I first started cooking this dish many years ago, I used only green bell peppers, but today I often use colorful red and yellow peppers to add visual appeal.

1. In a sauté pan or skillet large enough to hold all of the pasta after it is cooked, sauté the peppers in the oil over medium heat for 1 minute while stirring. Cover the pan and cook for 3 minutes longer, stirring at least once.

2. Add the onion, parsley, tomatoes, garlic, and basil, breaking up the tomatoes with the back of a wooden spoon. Bring the sauce to a lively simmer and cook for 15 to 20 minutes, until most of the liquid in the pan has evaporated. Season with salt and pepper.

3. About 10 minutes before the sauce is done, bring the water to a boil, add salt to taste, and cook the pasta until not quite al dente, (it will cook a bit more in the sauce)— about 8 to 10 minutes.

4. Drain the pasta and add it to the sauce. Cook and stir gently over medium heat for 1 to 2 minutes. Add the cheese and stir again. Serve at once.

1 cup cut-up red bell peppers in 1-inch squares
1 cup cut-up yellow bell peppers in 1-inch squares
2 tablespoons extra-virgin olive oil
¼ cup chopped yellow onion
¼ cup flat-leaf parsley
1 28-ounce can plum tomatoes, with juice
2 cloves garlic, chopped fine
¼ cup torn fresh basil leaves or 1 teaspoon dried, crumbled
Salt and freshly ground black pepper to taste
6 quarts water
¾ pound rigatoni
½ cup freshly grated Parmesan cheese

Serves 4
Calories: 490 per serving

Ziti con Broccoli e Ceci

(Ziti with Broccoli and Chick-Peas)

There are only four major ingredients in this dish, but the taste belies that simplicity. In my mother's kitchen chick-peas, a filling and inexpensive commodity, were used in many different ways, quite frequently in salads and pasta dishes. This dish is at its best when the broccoli florets are small, so cut larger pieces down to size if necessary. Make the sauce while the pasta is cooking and you'll be eating healthfully and well in less than 15 minutes.

¾ pound (about 1½ cups) broccoli florets with no stems

6 quarts water

Salt to taste

¾ pound ziti or mostaccioli

5 tablespoons extra-virgin olive oil

2 cloves garlic, sliced thin

1 15-ounce can chick-peas, drained and rinsed

Freshly ground black pepper to taste

⅛ teaspoon crushed red pepper flakes (optional)

1. Place the broccoli in a steamer basket over boiling water. Cover and steam the broccoli for 5 to 6 minutes, until it is cooked through yet still firm. Plunge the broccoli into cold water to stop the cooking and set the color. Set aside.

2. Bring the water to a boil, add salt, and cook the pasta until it is al dente, about 8 to 10 minutes.

3. While pasta is cooking, make the sauce. In a sauté pan or skillet large enough to hold all the cooked pasta, warm 2 tablespoons of olive oil over medium-high heat. Add the garlic and cook and stir until the garlic turns a toasty brown (do not burn), pressing down on it with the back of a wooden spoon—about 2 to 3 minutes. Discard the garlic.

4. Reduce the heat to medium, add the chick-peas to the pan, and cook and stir for 1 minute. Add the cooked pasta, the broccoli, and the red pepper flakes if desired. Cook and stir gently over medium heat for 2 minutes. Drizzle the remaining olive oil over the pasta. Serve at once.

Serves 4
Calories: 564 per serving

Farfalle con Rapini

(Farfalle with Rapini)

The exquisite slightly bitter flavor and soft yet crunchy texture of rapini (also called *broccoli rabe* and *cima di rapa*) will work with any sturdy pasta. While the vegetable is more widely available than ever, unfortunately it's not during the summer months. I have chosen farfalle, or butterfly pasta, a pasta with more eating surface, to contrast with the delicate nature of the rapini. Rigatoni would also work. Roasted red peppers add another dimension.

1. Bring the water to a boil, add salt, and cook the pasta until it is al dente, about 8 to 10 minutes.

2. While the pasta is cooking, combine the oil, garlic, red pepper flakes, sun-dried tomatoes, and cooked rapini in a sauté pan or skillet large enough to hold all of the cooked pasta. Over medium-high heat, cook and stir for 3 minutes. Add the pasta and stir to combine. Turn the heat to medium and cook and stir for 2 more minutes. Add salt to taste and 3 or 4 grinds of pepper. Serve at once.

Note: One pound of rapini, trimmed, becomes about 1 cup after cooking if the rapini is cooked in water. If the rapini is steamed, 1 pound of fresh rapini becomes about ¾ pound.

To prepare the rapini for cooking, cut off 3 to 4 inches of the stem and wash in a bowl of cold water, changing the water twice. Cook the rapini in boiling water for 18 to 20 minutes or steam it over low heat in a covered pot using the water clinging to the leaves from washing plus 1 cup of water.

6 quarts water
Salt to taste
¾ pound farfalle
2 tablespoons extra-virgin olive oil
1 clove garlic, chopped fine
⅛ teaspoon crushed red pepper flakes
1 cup drained oil-packed sun-dried tomatoes, cut into ⅛-inch strips
5 cups cooked rapini, chopped coarse (see note)
Freshly ground black pepper to taste

Serves 4
Calories: 548 per serving

Spaghetti alla Salsa Fresca Pomodoro

(Spaghetti with Fresh Tomato Sauce)

Use only very ripe plum tomatoes and fresh basil (no substitutes) for this dish and you will be amply rewarded. If you use a short pasta such as penne or fusilli, the dish can be served at room temperature.

1 tablespoon balsamic vinegar
3 tablespoons virgin olive oil
Salt and freshly ground black
   pepper to taste
1½ pounds plum tomatoes,
   peeled, seeded, and chopped
   coarse (see Index)
½ cup torn fresh basil leaves
4 quarts water
6 ounces spaghetti
Freshly grated Parmesan
   cheese for serving (optional)

1. In a small bowl, whisk together the vinegar and oil. Season with salt and pepper. Stir the tomatoes and basil into the oil and vinegar mixture.

2. Bring the water to a boil, add salt to taste, and cook the spaghetti until al dente, about 8 to 10 minutes. Drain well and place it in a serving bowl. Add the sauce to the pasta and toss quickly. Serve grated Parmesan cheese on the side if desired.

Serves 2
Calories: 575 per serving

Fusilli Sicilia

(Fusilli in the Style of Sicily)

The dominant flavor of olives and olive oil always signifies a dish peculiar to southern Italy. The fragrance of olive oil permeates this dish. Serve it hot or serve it cold, but make sure you have plenty to serve, because its full flavor is irresistible. The sauce should be of coarse texture, so do not process it too much.

....

1. In a food processor, blend the olives, peppers, and olive oil into a coarse puree. Season with salt and pepper.

2. Bring the water to a boil, add salt to taste, and cook the pasta until al dente, about 6 to 8 minutes. Drain well and put the pasta in a large serving bowl and toss it with the dressing. Pass grated Parmesan cheese separately if desired.

Serves 4
Calories: 514 per serving

¼ cup green olives, pitted
½ cup oil-cured black olives, pitted
¾ cup chopped peeled roasted red bell peppers (jarred peppers are fine)
¼ cup extra-virgin olive oil
Salt and freshly ground pepper to taste
6 quarts water
¾ pound fusilli or similar short pasta
Freshly grated Parmesan cheese for serving (optional)

Ziti con Carciofi

(Ziti with Artichokes)

Italians eat artichokes the way Americans eat popcorn. I came upon this impromptu dish on many occasions in my Aunt Rosie's kitchen (on my frequent visits she would insist that I eat *before* I went home to eat). While she usually used sliced fresh plum tomatoes rather than sun-dried tomatoes, the contrasting textures and flavors are as pleasing in this version as in Aunt Rosie's.

....

1 10-ounce package frozen
    artichoke hearts
6 quarts water
Salt to taste
¾ pound ziti
2 tablespoons virgin olive oil
2 cloves garlic, minced
½ cup drained oil-packed
    sun-dried tomatoes,
    chopped
½ cup fresh bread crumbs
Freshly ground black pepper
    to taste
Freshly grated Parmesan
    cheese for serving (optional)

1. Cook the artichokes according to package directions and reserve.

2. Boil the water in a large pot, add salt, and cook the ziti until al dente, about 8 to 10 minutes.

3. Prepare the sauce while the pasta is cooking. In a skillet or sauté pan large enough to hold all the pasta after it is cooked, warm the oil over medium heat for 1 minute. Add the garlic and sun-dried tomatoes and cook and stir for 2 to 3 minutes. Add the bread crumbs and artichokes and cook and stir gently for 2 minutes or until the artichoke hearts are heated through.

4. Drain the pasta well and put it in the pan with the artichokes. Over low heat, toss gently to combine. Serve at once with grated Parmesan cheese on the side if desired.

Serves 4 to 6
Calories: 467 per serving

Pasta with Seafood

Spaghetti con Scampi

(Spaghetti with Shrimp)

With the sauce requiring no more than the time it takes to cook the pasta, this can be an almost impromptu affair. The fact that it has hardly any fat makes it inviting as a "weekly regular." A small amount of red pepper flakes added to the sauce gives it just the right picante flavor.

....

4 quarts water
Salt to taste
¾ pound spaghetti
2 large cloves garlic, sliced
   lengthwise
1 tablespoon extra-virgin olive
   oil
2 28-ounce cans plum
   tomatoes, 1 drained
½ cup dry white wine
1 teaspoon dried thyme,
   crumbled
16 large (about ¾ pound)
   shrimp, peeled and deveined
½ teaspoon crushed red
   pepper flakes (optional)
Freshly ground black pepper
   to taste

1. Bring the water to a boil in a large pot, add salt, and cook the pasta until al dente, about 8 to 10 minutes.

2. Meanwhile, make the sauce. In a large sauté pan or skillet set over medium heat, gently sauté the garlic in the oil until it turns toasty brown, 2 to 3 minutes. Take the pan off the heat and discard the garlic.

3. Add the tomatoes, white wine, and thyme. Place the pan back over medium-high heat and bring the sauce to a steady simmer. Cook and stir for about 6 minutes, breaking up the tomatoes with a wooden spoon, until most of the liquid has evaporated. Add the shrimp to the pan, turn the heat to medium-low, cover the pan, and simmer for 4 minutes.

4. Put all of the cooked pasta into the pan with the sauce, toss, and combine thoroughly. Add the crushed red pepper flakes if desired and a small amount of pepper and combine thoroughly.

5. Divide the pasta among four heated serving bowls and arrange three shrimp across the top of each dish. Serve at once.

Serves 4
Calories: 523 per serving

Linguine alle Vongole

(Linguine with White Clam Sauce)

A quick and tasty pasta dish that can be brought to the table in less than 20 minutes. The only salt in the dish is that used in the pasta water.

....

1. In a saucepan set over medium heat, sauté the garlic in the oil until it is lightly browned, about 3 to 4 minutes. Discard the garlic.

2. Drain the juices from the minced clams into a measuring cup, reserving the chopped clams. Add enough bottled clam juice to make 1½ cups. Put the clam juice into the saucepan set over low heat. Add the parsley, thyme, red pepper flakes, and pepper.

3. While the sauce is heating, bring the water to a boil in a large pot, add salt to taste, and cook the linguine until al dente, about 6 to 8 minutes. Drain the pasta and put it in a large serving bowl.

4. Increase the heat and bring the clam sauce to a simmer. Off the heat, add the reserved minced clams and give the sauce a good stir. Pour the clam sauce over the pasta and toss it gently and quickly. Serve at once.

2 cloves garlic, sliced
2 tablespoons virgin olive oil
2 6½-ounce cans minced
   clams
Bottled clam juice
2 tablespoons finely chopped
   flat-leaf parsley
1 teaspoon dried thyme,
   crumbled
⅛ teaspoon crushed red
   pepper flakes
Freshly ground black pepper
   to taste
4 quarts water
Salt to taste
¾ pound linguine

Serves 4
Calories: 452 per serving

Variation: To change the white sauce to a red sauce, add 1 cup tomato puree in step 2.

Pasta e Vongole Subito

(Quick Pasta and Clams)

This is another version of the well-known linguine with clam sauce. However, in this version fresh clams are used. Would that they were the tiny clams—true vongole—used in Italy. Nevertheless, if you buy the tiniest littleneck clams available, your finished dish will be most satisfying. Use a simple dry white wine such as Orvieto or Soave to make the sauce. Serve the pasta and clams in large soup bowls with crusty Italian bread for sopping up the delicious sauce.

....

6 quarts water
½ cup dry white wine
¼ cup extra-virgin olive oil
24 littleneck clams, scrubbed well
Salt to taste
¾ pound linguine or thin spaghetti
2 cloves garlic, minced
¼ cup finely chopped flat-leaf parsley
1 teaspoon dried thyme, crumbled
Freshly ground black pepper to taste
Chopped flat-leaf parsley for garnish

1. In a large pot, bring 2 cups of the water, the wine, and the oil to a gentle boil. Reduce the heat to medium-high and add the clams. Cover the pot and cook until all the clams open—6 to 8 minutes—shaking the pan gently halfway through. Discard any clams that do not open.

2. Meanwhile, bring the remaining gallon of water to a boil in another large pot, add salt, and cook the pasta according to package directions, until it is al dente.

3. Sprinkle the garlic, ¼ cup parsley, and thyme over the clams in the pot. Stir the clams and sauce thoroughly but gently. (The clams and sauce can be kept for about 5 minutes over low heat if necessary, but do not cover the pot.) Season with salt and pepper.

4. Divide the cooked pasta among four bowls. Arrange six clams around the edge of the pasta in each bowl. Spoon equal amounts of sauce among the four bowls. Garnish with chopped parsley.

Serves 4
Calories: 527 per serving

Fettuccine con Capesante e Scarola

(Fettuccine with Scallops and Escarole)

In this luscious pasta dish the sweet and delicate flavor of the scallops nicely offset the slightly bitter taste of the escarole. If you're using sea scallops, cut the large ones into smaller pieces. Do not use any cheese with this dish; it destroys the delicate balance of flavors.

1. In a skillet or sauté pan large enough to hold all the cooked pasta, brown the garlic in 2 tablespoons oil over medium-high heat, about 3 to 4 minutes. Discard the garlic.

2. Raise the heat to high, add the scallops, and sauté for 1 minute. Add 1 tablespoon olive oil if necessary to prevent sticking.

3. Add the white wine and cook and stir gently until the alcohol has evaporated—about 1 minute.

4. Reduce the heat to medium-low and add the clam juice, thyme, and escarole. Cook and stir for 2 minutes or until the escarole wilts. The dish can be prepared to this point and held for about 1 hour.

5. Bring the water to a boil in a large pot, add salt, and cook the fettuccine until al dente, about 6 to 8 minutes. Drain quickly (some water left on the pasta is advisable, so don't drain the pasta too thoroughly).

6. Return the sauce to the stove over medium heat. Dump all the cooked pasta into the pan and stir and cook for about 1 minute. Serve at once on heated plates.

2 cloves garlic, sliced
2–3 tablespoons extra-virgin olive oil
1 pound scallops
¼ cup dry white wine
1 cup bottled clam juice
2 teaspoons dried thyme, crumbled
½ pound escarole, washed thoroughly and chopped coarse
6 quarts water
Salt to taste
1 pound fettuccine

Serves 4 to 6
Calories: 420 per serving

Spaghetti al Salmone Affumicato

(Spaghettini with Smoked Salmon)

Spaghettini, the slim version of spaghetti, is combined with silky smoked salmon and zucchini in a light cream sauce. I cut a lot of the fat out of my original recipe for this dish by substituting skim milk for half the normal amount of heavy cream. This is my thoroughly modern version of a dish that my mother often made during Lent. She used baccalà, or dried salt cod, instead of salmon. The smoky, intense interest is retained with the use of salmon, but without the lengthy preparation required of dried cod. Cheese does not complement this dish; do *not* pass the Parmesan.

2 tablespoons unsalted butter

2 tablespoons extra-virgin olive oil

2 garlic cloves, minced

½ pound (about 2 small) zucchini, halved lengthwise, seeds removed, and sliced thin crosswise

½ cup whipping cream

½ cup skim milk

1 teaspoon dried thyme, crumbled

1 tablespoon fresh lemon juice

⅓ cup frozen peas, soaked in hot water for 10 minutes

Salt and freshly ground white pepper to taste

6 quarts water

¾ pound spaghettini, vermicelli, or angel hair

6 ounces smoked salmon, cut into ¼-inch strips

1. In a sauté pan large enough to hold all the cooked pasta, melt the butter with the oil over medium heat. Add the garlic and zucchini and sauté until the zucchini softens slightly—about 2 minutes.

2. Add the cream and skim milk and simmer until the sauce thickens slightly—about 6 minutes.

3. Add the thyme, lemon juice, and peas; simmer for 4 minutes. Season with salt and pepper.

4. Meanwhile, bring the water to a boil in a large pot, add salt, and cook the pasta until al dente, according to package directions. Drain quickly and add it to the sauté pan with the sauce. Turn the heat to high, stir, and simmer the pasta and sauce for 2 minutes.

5. Divide the pasta among four heated pasta bowls and arrange the strips of salmon over the pasta. Serve at once.

Serves 4
Calories: 611 per serving

Homemade Pasta

In my cooking school I conduct hands-on classes in which students learn to make many different styles of pasta. Some of the pasta preparations are time-consuming. Ravioli, for example, calls for making the pasta and rolling it to the proper thinness before the stuffing and cutting are done. Many people can't find the time for all of that work, so in the following recipe I use a very acceptable substitute, one that cuts the time by more than half: wonton skins.

Ravioli Imbottiti di Pollo, Spinaci, e Peperoni Arrostiti

(Ravioli with Chicken, Spinach, and Roasted Peppers)

The only secret to working effectively with wonton skins for forming ravioli is water; the skins must be brushed liberally with water, or they will fall apart while boiling. There are two sizes of wonton skins: 6-inch and 3-inch. Either size works just fine.

Here is one example of a tasty stuffing for ravioli, or use your favorite. This filling can be made up to 1 day ahead and held in the refrigerator. And the ravioli can be frozen, so I like to make enough for several meals.

1 10-ounce package frozen chopped spinach

1½ pounds skinless, bone-in chicken breasts

½ cup finely chopped peeled roasted red peppers (jarred peppers are fine)

¼ cup freshly grated Parmesan cheese

Salt and freshly ground black pepper to taste

About ½ package 3-inch wonton skins

1. Cook the spinach according to package directions. Drain, squeeze dry, and chop fine. Set aside.

2. Put the chicken in a 3- to 4-quart pot and cover with cold water. Bring to a boil and poach until the chicken is cooked through, 12 to 15 minutes. Remove the chicken from the water and reserve about ½ cup of the poaching liquid. When the chicken is cool enough to handle, pick the meat off the bones and chop it fine. You will have about 1½ cups.

3. In a mixing bowl, combine the cooked spinach, cooked chicken, roasted peppers, and cheese. Blend thoroughly and season with salt and pepper.

4. Form the ravioli by laying two of the wonton skins on the kitchen counter and brushing each liberally on one side with water. Put about 1 heaped tablespoon of the filling on one of the skins, place the other skin over the filling, and press down firmly with the tips of your fingers to seal the edges.

Run a pastry cutter around all sides. Place the ravioli on a platter or a baking sheet or pan large enough to fit in the freezer (if you plan to freeze them). Proceed until all the filling has been used up. Cook at once for about 2 minutes in a large pot of boiling water or allow to dry for up to 1 hour before freezing. If frozen, cook without thawing for about 4 to 5 minutes.

Makes 26 to 28 3-inch ravioli
Calories: 47 per serving (1 3-inch ravioli)

To Roast and Peel Red Peppers

While the jarred peppers are perfectly acceptable, you might want to take advantage of the late-summer bounty and roast and peel your own.

Push the stem end of the pepper into the pepper and then pull it out intact and discard. Cut the pepper in half lengthwise and remove the seeds. Push down hard with the palm of your hand to flatten each half. Place the pepper halves on a baking sheet and place it under a preheated broiler about 3 to 4 inches from the heat. When the skin on the peppers chars and turns black, about 7 minutes, remove the peppers from the oven, put them in a metal bowl, and cover the bowl tightly with plastic wrap (this steaming will make it easier to remove the charred skin later). After about 30 minutes (up to an hour), remove the peppers from the bowl and peel or scrape the skin off the peppers. The peppers can now be used in various recipes using roasted peppers, or they can be placed in a jar with olive oil to cover and stored in a cool, dark place for up to a month. If you are planning to use the peppers within 3 to 4 days, simply put them in a covered bowl in the refrigerator.

Pasta al Peperoni Arrostiti

(Roasted Red Pepper Pasta)

Once this pasta dough has been made, it can be cut into various shapes. In my cooking school we use a manual pasta machine to roll and cut the dough.

....

1. In a food processor fitted with the steel blade, process the peppers, semolina flour, and salt until well combined. With the machine running, drizzle almost all of the water through the feed tube. The dough should form a ball and ride around the work bowl. If the dough doesn't ball up, add a little more water. If the dough feels sticky, add a small amount of flour.

2. Turn the dough out of the work bowl and knead by hand for 1 minute. The dough is now ready to use for making various styles of pasta.

3. After rolling and cutting, cook at once in a large pot of boiling water for 2 minutes or dry for 5 to 6 hours and then store in an airtight container (do not refrigerate). Cook dried pasta for 4 to 5 minutes. Serve with sauce of your choice; try *Pomodoro Verdure* or one of the pesto sauces (see Index).

½ cup roasted red peppers (jarred peppers are fine), patted dry
2 cups semolina flour
Pinch of salt
About ½ cup warm water

Makes 1 pound of pasta
Calories: 204 per 2-ounce serving

Gnocchi con Ricotta

(Dumplings with Ricotta Cheese)

Gnocchi, aka cavatelli, is one of the benchmarks that I use to evaluate how well a restaurant makes homemade pasta. On Sunday mornings during my childhood the kitchen table was covered with cavatelli waiting to go into a pot of boiling water. Of course the job of rolling the nubbins of dough across the tines of a fork was given to my brothers and me, but we always managed to make short work of 3 or 4 pounds of cavatelli.

This recipe makes a lot of gnocchi, but they freeze well, so you will have more to look forward to at another time.

....

1 15-ounce carton low-fat ricotta cheese, well drained
2 large eggs, lightly beaten
¼ cup freshly grated Parmesan cheese
About 3 cups unbleached all-purpose flour
Freshly ground black pepper to taste
Pinch of freshly grated nutmeg

1. Place the ricotta, eggs, and Parmesan in a food processor fitted with the steel blade. Process for about 30 seconds to combine.

2. Add 2 cups of the flour and turn on the machine to combine. With the machine running, add more flour through the feed tube, about ¼ cup at a time, until the dough forms a ball and comes away from the sides of the bowl. Add the pepper and nutmeg. The dough should be soft but not sticky.

3. Turn the dough out of the bowl onto a lightly floured surface and knead gently for 2 minutes. The dough can be used at once to make gnocchi; it can be refrigerated for up to 24 hours, tightly covered; or it can be wrapped and frozen for later use.

4. To form gnocchi, cut off a small piece of dough and roll it firmly between the palms of your hands, then lightly with the palms of your hands on the work surface, to form a "rope" or cylinder about ¼ inch in diameter. Cut the cylinder into pieces about ½ inch long. Roll each piece across the tines of a fork, pressing firmly so that the dough is marked

with ridges and a small pocket is formed. Place the rolled gnocchi on clean kitchen towels or paper towels, cover, and let dry for 15 to 20 minutes.

5. Cook the gnocchi in plenty of boiling salted water or freeze. The gnocchi are done 30 seconds after they rise to the surface of the boiling water. If frozen, cook unthawed for 6 to 8 minutes. Serve with *Salsa Marinara* or *Pomodoro Verdure* (see Index).

Makes about 2¼ pounds of gnocchi, serving 6 to 8
Calories: 208 per serving

Pasta al Pepe Nero

(Black Pepper Pasta)

1½ cups semolina flour
2 scant teaspoons freshly
   ground black pepper
Pinch of salt
About ½ cup warm water

Follow the directions for Roasted Red Pepper Pasta (preceding recipe). Try *Salsa Marinara* or *Pomodoro Verdure* (see Index) with the cooked pasta.

Makes 1 pound of pasta
Calories: 152 per 2-ounce serving

Additional Sauces

Pomodoro Verdure

(Tomato and Vegetable Sauce)

Here is a large-quantity tomato sauce that is a snap to make, has practically no fat, and freezes well. Try to use a canned tomato puree with no added salt. Better yet, use fresh plum tomatoes in the summer. Peel and seed the tomatoes and process them in a food processor in two or three batches to form a smooth puree. Use the sauce for pasta or any dish (an eggplant parmigiana, for example) that requires a simple tomato sauce.

3 large carrots, scraped and chopped

3 large ribs celery (with a few leaves), chopped

1 medium-size yellow onion, chopped

6 cups tomato puree or 6-7 pounds fresh plum tomatoes, peeled, seeded, and pureed in a food processor (see Index)

1 cup water (omit if using fresh tomatoes)

2 large cloves garlic, crushed

2 tablespoons virgin olive oil

1 bay leaf

Salt and freshly ground black pepper to taste

1. In a food processor fitted with the steel blade, process the carrots, celery, and onion until a smooth puree is formed. Transfer the puree to a 3- to 4-quart heavy pot.

2. Add the tomato puree to the pot along with the water, garlic, olive oil, and bay leaf and simmer the sauce for 1 hour. Season with salt and pepper. Discard the bay leaf before using.

Makes 6 cups, enough for about 2 pounds pasta

Calories: 88 per ½-cup serving

To Peel and Seed
Fresh Plum Tomatoes

Make an X in the stem end of the tomato. Plunge the tomatoes into rapidly boiling water for about 1 to 2 minutes (the riper the tomato, the less time required). Scoop the tomatoes from the boiling water and put them in a bowl.

When the tomatoes are cool enough to handle, slip off the skin, cut the tomato in half lengthwise, and scoop out the seeds with the tip of a small spoon.

Salsa Bolognese al Tacchino

(Meatless Bolognese Sauce)

Other than ground turkey replacing ground beef, this is a classic sauce Bolognese. The sauce is great with pasta of any shape or size. It can be made ahead and refrigerated for up to 4 days. It also freezes well.

....

2 tablespoons virgin olive oil
¼ cup chopped yellow onion
1 pound fresh ground turkey
1 teaspoon fennel seed
¼ cup skim milk
1 28-ounce can plum
   tomatoes, with juice
3 tablespoons chopped flat-
   leaf parsley
2 teaspoons dried oregano,
   crumbled
½ cup Chicken Stock (see
   Index) or lower-salt canned
   chicken broth
Salt and freshly ground black
   pepper to taste

1. Heat the oil in a heavy 4- to 5-quart pot over medium heat. Add the onion and cook and stir for 3 minutes. Add the ground turkey and continue to stir and cook until the turkey is just cooked through but not browned, 3 to 4 minutes. Add the fennel seed and milk and cook and stir for 2 minutes.

2. Add the tomatoes, parsley, oregano, and stock. Bring the sauce to a boil. Reduce the heat to low and simmer the sauce, uncovered, stirring occasionally, for 1 hour. Season with salt and pepper.

Makes about 1 quart, enough for about 1½ pounds pasta
Calories: 140 per ½-cup serving

Alici alla Moda Bruno

(Anchovy Sauce)

My roots are in Reggio Calabria, where alici is a dish made with baked fresh anchovies that have been seasoned with garlic, oil, and capers. I have turned the dish into a fragrant sauce of great versatility. It can be used with artichokes, asparagus, or boiled potatoes and as a sauce for a thin pasta such as capelli d'angelo or capellini.

....

Place everything except the olive oil, salt, and pepper in a food processor fitted with the steel blade. Process with short pulses until a coarse mixture is formed. With the machine running, add the olive oil in a steady stream. The sauce should be somewhat liquid. If it is too thick, add a tablespoon or more of water to thin it. Transfer the sauce to a mixing bowl and season with salt and pepper.

Makes about ½ cup, enough for about ¼ pound pasta
Calories: 299 per ¼-cup serving

3 cloves garlic, minced
½ cup fresh bread crumbs
1 tablespoon drained capers, rinsed
4 anchovy fillets, rinsed
1 teaspoon dried oregano, crumbled
3 tablespoons chopped flat-leaf parsley
⅛ teaspoon crushed red pepper flakes
¼ cup extra-virgin olive oil
Salt and freshly ground black pepper to taste

Salsa Marinara

(Marinara Sauce)

2 tablespoons virgin olive oil
½ cup chopped yellow onion
3 cloves garlic, minced
¼ cup chopped flat-leaf
   parsley
2 28-ounce cans plum
   tomatoes, 1 drained
2 teaspoons dried oregano,
   crumbled
2 teaspoons dried basil,
   crumbled
½ teaspoon sugar
Salt and freshly ground black
   pepper to taste

1. In a 3- to 4-quart saucepan set over medium heat, warm the oil for 1 minute. Add the onion, garlic, and parsley. Cook and stir for 2 minutes. Add the tomatoes and crush them with the back of a wooden spoon. Add the oregano and the basil and stir well to combine.

2. Bring the sauce to a gentle boil, reduce the heat, and simmer, uncovered, for about 1 hour. Season with salt and pepper. This sauce freezes well.

Makes about 6 cups, enough for 2 pounds pasta
Calories: 52 per ½-cup serving

Pesto Genovese

(Basil, Garlic, and Pine Nut Sauce)

Just before being used, the pesto should be thinned with hot water (or water in which the pasta is being cooked). This is a classic recipe with a little less cheese and oil than usually called for.

Place the basil, garlic, cheese, and 3 tablespoons of the pine nuts in a food processor fitted with the steel blade. Pulse the machine 10 to 12 times or until the ingredients are thoroughly combined. With the motor running, slowly add the olive oil. Process until smooth. Season with salt and pepper and stir in the remaining pine nuts.

Makes 1½ to 2 cups, enough for about 1 pound pasta
Calories: 247 per ¼-cup serving

2 cups loosely packed fresh basil leaves
2 cloves garlic, peeled
2 tablespoons freshly grated Parmesan cheese
2 tablespoons grated Romano cheese
¼ cup pine nuts
½ cup plus 1 tablespoon extra-virgin olive oil
Salt and freshly ground black pepper to taste

Trito di Olive Agli Aromi

(Olive Pesto)

Use this sauce on pasta or to spread on grilled or toasted Italian bread (bruschetta or crostini; see Index).

....

½ cup pimiento-stuffed green olives, rinsed
½ cup oil-cured black olives, pitted
¼ cup pine nuts
2 cloves garlic, peeled
1 cup flat-leaf parsley leaves
¼ cup extra-virgin olive oil
2 tablespoons freshly grated Parmesan cheese

Put the olives, the pine nuts, the garlic, and parsley in a food processor fitted with the steel blade. Process until smooth. With the machine running, add the olive oil in a steady stream. Transfer the sauce to a bowl and blend in the Parmesan cheese.

Makes about 1½ cups, enough for about 1 pound pasta
Calories: 178 per ¼-cup serving

Salsa di Noci

(Walnut Sauce)

An excellent sauce for ravioli, but it marries nicely, too, with a short pasta such as penne or mostaccioli.

....

Put all the ingredients except the olive oil, salt, and pepper in a food processor fitted with the steel blade. Process for about 30 seconds or until the ingredients are combined. With the machine running, add the olive oil in a steady stream. Season with salt and pepper. Before using the sauce on pasta, you may need to thin it a bit; use hot water from the pasta pot in that case.

Makes about 1½ cups, enough for at least 1 pound pasta
Calories: 218 per ¼-cup serving

½ cup walnut pieces
¼ cup pine nuts
2 cloves garlic, peeled
¼ cup chopped flat-leaf parsley
½ cup low-fat ricotta cheese
¼ cup freshly grated Parmesan cheese
¼ cup virgin olive oil
Salt and freshly ground black pepper to taste

Sugo Calamari

(Squid Sauce)

An assertive and texturally interesting sauce for pasta, especially a thinner pasta such as linguine.

....

About 1 pound squid, cleaned,
   rinsed under cold water,
   and patted dry with paper
   towels
¼ cup virgin olive oil
2 cloves garlic, minced
2 cups peeled, seeded, and
   chopped fresh or drained
   canned plum tomatoes (see
   Index)
¼ teaspoon crushed red
   pepper flakes
¼ cup chopped flat-leaf
   parsley
½ teaspoon dried thyme,
   crumbled
Salt and freshly ground black
   pepper to taste

1. Slice the body sac of the squid into rings about ⅛ inch wide. Set aside.

2. In a skillet or sauté pan set over medium heat, warm the oil for 1 minute. Add the garlic and squid rings and cook and stir for 1 minute more. Add the tomatoes, red pepper flakes, parsley, and thyme. Simmer the sauce, uncovered, stirring occasionally, for 20 to 25 minutes or until the squid is tender. Season with salt and pepper.

Makes 1½ to 2 cups, enough for about 1 pound pasta
Calories: 168 per ¼-cup serving

I cannot recall even once when I was growing up that my mother made a cold pasta salad. Pasta (she called it "macaroni," never pasta) was served with a sauce that was hot, not cold. Pasta went into a soup or broth, but it was never served cold. That was the unwritten rule around our house, so it took me quite some time to accept the idea that pasta could be good cooked and cooled—that it could take on salad status.

Status may be too soft a word these days, since I note that pasta bars and antipasto bars featuring cold (*room-temperature* would be a better description) pasta dishes are becoming a popular restaurant trend in America. (It will be a while before Italy embraces this concept, you can be sure.)

Pasta salads do have an important place in the way we cook and eat these days. The idea that the salad can be made hours (even a day) ahead is comforting. Even more exciting is the fact that pasta salads vastly expand the pasta possibilities—especially in the summer, when vegetables are at peak flavor. And the idea of toting a pasta salad to a concert or on a picnic is even more inviting, especially with these recipes, since none of them use any mayonnaise or cream, greatly lengthening the keeping time.

I find that a "short pasta" works better in pasta salads than a "long pasta" such as spaghetti or linguine. Also, children have an easier time (and get less messy) handling a short pasta.

COLD PASTA SALADS

Insalata di Ceci, Acini di Pepe e Finocchio

(Acini di Pepe and Chick-Peas with Fennel)

This cold pasta dish has some Sardinian influences and some that are from the south of Italy. The Sardinian influence is the smallest of pasta shapes. I use acini di pepe (peppercorn-shaped pasta) in place of fregola, which are tiny grains of pasta used mostly in a soup in Sardinian cooking. The southern influence is the chick-peas: there they are used extensively with pasta and in soups. If you can't locate acini de pepe pasta, use riso or small tubetti pasta. The entire dish can be made a day ahead and refrigerated. Take it from the refrigerator 1 hour before serving.

2 quarts water
Salt to taste
¾ cup (6 ounces) acini di pepe
1 teaspoon extra-virgin olive oil
2 cloves garlic, minced
½ cup (about 2 ounces) finely chopped prosciutto
1 16-ounce can chick-peas, drained and rinsed
1 28-ounce can plum tomatoes, drained and chopped coarse
1½-pound fennel bulb, halved lengthwise, cored, and sliced thin
2 tablespoons extra-virgin olive oil
Freshly ground black pepper to taste
¼ cup grated Romano cheese

1. Bring the water to a boil in a large pot, add salt, and cook the pasta until al dente—about 6 to 8 minutes. Drain it well and put it in a medium-size mixing bowl. Dress the pasta with 1 teaspoon extra-virgin olive oil and toss gently. Put the pasta in the refrigerator for about 1 hour to cool.

2. While the pasta is cooling, in a salad bowl, combine the garlic, prosciutto, chick-peas, tomatoes, and fennel. Add the 2 tablespoons extra-virgin olive oil and toss well. Season with salt and pepper. (This part of the pasta salad can be made ahead and refrigerated.)

3. Add the cooled pasta to the salad bowl and toss gently to combine. Sprinkle on the cheese if serving at once; otherwise, add it just before serving.

Serves 4 to 6
Calories: 276 per serving

Select Italian Cheeses

Parmigiano Reggiano: Its presence is the sine qua non of many Italian dishes. Made in small factories in the provinces of Bologna, Parma, Reggio Emilia, and Modena, true Parmesan cheese—Parmigiano Reggiano—is a beautiful straw color, a bit crumbly, and when freshly grated has a mellow, almost fruity flavor. When buying this great cheese, look for the golden-yellow rind stamped with the words *Parmigiano-Reggiano*. It is at peak flavor if cut to order from the cheese wheel rather than precut into wedges and wrapped in plastic. And it is at full flavor when freshly grated just before being used.

Domestic Parmesan does not have the same rich and nutty flavor as its imported progenitor, but considering that the price for domestic Parmesan is about half that of the imported, it should not be ruled out. Domestic Parmesan most often has a rind that is almost black. If the cheese just below the rind is a darker color than the rest, it means that the wedge is not at its freshest. Look for a wedge in which there are no color variations near the rind.

Pecorino Romano: Produced mostly in southern and central Italy, this hard grating cheese, made from sheep's milk, has a sharp, slightly salty flavor, a flavor much more robust than Parmesan. Domestic pecorino doesn't have the same sharp flavor as the imported, nevertheless, it is a very acceptable substitute and is most often labeled simply *Romano*.

Penne ai Peperoni Arrostiti e Pinoli

(Penne with Roasted Peppers and Toasted Pine Nuts)

The easy and quite acceptable way to complete this dish in short order is to use a 7-ounce jar of roasted red peppers. However, if you wish to bring in added color and a slightly fresher flavor, roast your own as described.

The two components—pasta and dressing—can be made up to a day ahead and refrigerated. Combine just before serving.

6 quarts water
Salt to taste
¾ pound penne or other
    tubular pasta such as ziti
    or mostaccioli
3 teaspoons extra-virgin olive
    oil
¼ cup pine nuts
1 clove garlic, minced
¼ cup virgin olive oil
½ cup thinly sliced red onion
1 7-ounce jar roasted red
    peppers, drained and
    chopped coarse or 1
    medium-size green and 1
    medium-size yellow bell
    pepper, roasted (see note)
    and chopped coarse
Freshly ground black pepper
    to taste

1. Bring the water to a boil in a large pot, add salt, and cook the pasta until al dente, according to package directions. Drain well and transfer to a mixing bowl. Toss with 2 teaspoons of the extra-virgin olive oil. Cover the bowl with plastic wrap and refrigerate for at least 1 hour.

2. Place the remaining teaspoon of extra-virgin olive oil and the pine nuts in a small nonstick frying pan over medium heat. Stir and cook until the pine nuts just begin to turn golden brown, about 3 minutes. Set aside.

3. In a large serving bowl, combine the garlic, virgin olive oil, onion, and peppers. Season with salt and pepper and toss well.

4. Add the cooled pasta to the bowl with the oil and garlic. Add the pine nuts. Toss well.

Note: Preheat the broiler. Cut the peppers in half lengthwise, core and seed them, and flatten each half with the palm of your hand. Place the peppers skin side up in one layer on a baking sheet close to the heat and cook them until the skin starts to blacken and blister. Place the peppers in a bowl and cover the bowl with plastic wrap to steam for 10 minutes, which helps to loosen their skin. Use the back of a knife to scrape away the charred skin.

Serves 4 to 6
Calories: 355 per serving

Rigatoni con Ceci e Broccoli

(Rigatoni with Chick-Peas and Broccoli)

The easy way to go about making this dish is to cook the pasta first and then prepare the tomatoes and broccoli. This work can be done several hours in advance. Once the pasta has cooled, the final assembly takes but minutes.

6 quarts water
Salt to taste
½ pound rigatoni
½ pound (about 1 cup)
   broccoli florets
2 tablespoons virgin olive oil
1 clove garlic, minced
¾ cup drained, canned chick-
   peas, rinsed
2 tablespoons chopped fresh
   basil or 1 teaspoon dried,
   crumbled
2 pounds fresh plum
   tomatoes, peeled, seeded,
   and crushed (see Index)
Freshly ground black pepper
   to taste

1. Bring the water to a boil in a large pot, add salt, and cook the pasta until al dente, about 8 to 10 minutes. Drain well and refrigerate for at least 1 hour.

2. Place the broccoli florets in a steamer over boiling water and steam for about 6 minutes or until just tender but not soft. Plunge the cooked broccoli into cold water to stop the cooking and set the color. Set aside.

3. In a large salad bowl, combine the olive oil with the garlic. Add the chick-peas and basil and toss well. Add the crushed plum tomatoes and the broccoli to the bowl. Add the cooled pasta and toss well. Season with salt and pepper. Serve at once or refrigerate for up to 2 hours.

Serves 4
Calories: 369 per serving

Pasta e Fagioli Freddo

(Cold Pasta and Beans)

This recipe transforms a classic dish of the Veneto region of Italy, a soup actually, into a wonderful cold pasta salad. And to make it easier, everything can be done ahead. Precede it with a simple green salad and follow it with gelato, and you have the perfect meal for a summer day.

....

1. Bring the water to a boil in a large pot, add salt, and cook the pasta until al dente, according to package directions. Drain well, transfer to a bowl, dress with the olive oil, and toss to coat the pasta. Refrigerate the pasta for at least 1 hour.

2. In a large salad bowl, combine the beans, tomatoes, oregano, rosemary, and red pepper flakes. Set aside. (This can be done an hour ahead.)

3. Add the cooled pasta to the bowl with the beans and tomatoes. Toss well. Add the cheese, salt, and pepper and toss once more. (The salad can be prepared up to 4 hours ahead and refrigerated.) Sprinkle on the chopped parsley and serve.

Serves 4
Calories: 360 per serving

6 quarts water
Salt to taste
½ pound tubetti or ditalini pasta
2 teaspoons extra-virgin olive oil
1½ cups drained canned cannellini beans, rinsed
1 28-ounce can plum tomatoes, drained and crushed
1 teaspoon dried oregano, crumbled
1 teaspoon dried rosemary, crumbled
⅛ teaspoon crushed red pepper flakes
2 tablespoons freshly grated Parmesan cheese
Freshly ground black pepper to taste
1 tablespoon chopped flat-leaf parsley for garnish

Ziti Puttanesca

(Hot and Spicy Ziti)

A classic hot pasta dish—*spaghetti puttanesca*—has undergone culinary surgery and emerged with a new look. Though served cold, and with a change in pasta shape, the dish is still spicy and fragrant.

....

6 quarts water
Salt to taste
¾ pound ziti or penne or
   other small tubular pasta
2 teaspoons extra-virgin olive
   oil
1 clove garlic, minced
1 28-ounce can plum
   tomatoes, drained and
   chopped coarse
6 anchovy fillets, rinsed and
   chopped (optional)
12 Kalamata olives or other
   oil-cured black olives, pitted
   and chopped
1 tablespoon drained capers,
   rinsed
⅛ teaspoon crushed red
   pepper flakes
1 tablespoon balsamic vinegar
2 tablespoons minced flat-leaf
   parsley
Freshly ground black pepper
   to taste

1. Bring the water to a boil in a large pot, add salt, and cook the pasta until al dente, according to package directions. Drain well and transfer to a large bowl. Dress the pasta with the olive oil and toss well to coat. Refrigerate the pasta, covered, for at least 1 hour.

2. In a large salad bowl, combine the remaining ingredients and toss well.

3. Add the cooled pasta to the bowl with the sauce and toss to coat the pasta. Let the pasta sit for 1 hour before serving. Or refrigerate the pasta and the sauce for up to 4 hours and combine the two an hour before serving.

_____

Serves 4
Calories: 402 per serving

Fusilli al Pollo con Peperoni

(Fusilli with Chicken and Peppers)

If you don't have the time to roast the peppers, use roasted red bell peppers that come in a jar or bottle. In fact, at certain times of the year it is less expensive to use the bottled peppers, and they will not compromise the flavor of the dish.

Each component of the dish—cooking the pasta, poaching the chicken, and roasting the peppers—can be done several hours ahead.

....

1. Bring the water to a boil in a large pot, add salt, and cook the pasta until al dente, about 6 to 8 minutes. Drain well and toss with the stock. Refrigerate, covered, for at least 1 hour.

2. Wash the chicken breasts under cold water and place them in a pot of cold water. Bring the water to a boil, lower the heat, and simmer, uncovered, until the chicken is cooked through, 10 to 12 minutes. Refrigerate the chicken for about 1 hour, then cut it into bite-size strips.

3. In a large salad bowl, combine the pasta, chicken, and peppers. Add the olive oil and vinegar and toss to combine. Add the oregano and pepper and toss once more. The dish can be served at once or held at room temperature for up to 1 hour.

Serves 4
Calories: 434 per serving

6 quarts water
Salt to taste
1 pound fusilli
½ cup Chicken Stock (see Index) or lower-salt canned chicken broth
¾ pound boneless, skinless chicken breasts
1 roasted red pepper, peeled and cut into strips, and 1 roasted green pepper, peeled and cut into strips (see Index), or 1 7-ounce jar roasted red bell peppers, drained
¼ cup extra-virgin olive oil
1 tablespoon balsamic vinegar
1 teaspoon dried oregano, crumbled
Freshly ground black pepper to taste

Farfalle con Carciofi e Pomodori Secchi

(Farfalle with Artichoke Hearts and Sun-Dried Tomatoes)

I am a big fan of frozen artichoke hearts, especially for salads and pasta salads, since the work of cleaning fresh artichokes can be most onerous. Also, frozen artichoke hearts offer a better value. That's the practical side of this dish. On the enjoyment end, the combination of sun-dried tomatoes, artichokes, and pasta is quite lavish. Other interesting tastes can be added—black olives, chick-peas, even cubes of cooked potatoes.

....

3 quarts water
Salt to taste
10 ounces farfalle
½ cup drained oil-packed
    sun-dried tomatoes,
    chopped
2 tablespoons extra-virgin
    olive oil
1 teaspoon balsamic vinegar
8–10 fresh basil leaves
⅛ teaspoon salt
4–5 grinds of black pepper
1 9-ounce package frozen
    artichoke hearts, steamed
    according to package
    directions, cooled, and each
    piece cut in half
2 tablespoons freshly grated
    Parmesan cheese
¼ cup chopped flat-leaf
    parsley

1. Bring the water to a boil in a large pot, add salt, and cook the pasta until al dente, about 8 to 10 minutes. Drain it well and put it in a large serving bowl. Set aside.

2. In a food processor fitted with the steel blade, process the tomatoes, oil, vinegar, and basil until a smooth puree is formed. Mix in the salt and pepper.

3. Toss the tomato mixture with the pasta. Add the reserved artichokes and Parmesan cheese and toss gently to combine. Garnish with chopped parsley. Refrigerate for at least 2 hours before serving.

Serves 4
Calories: 275 per serving

In the Italian scheme of eating, dessert more often than not involves fruit, either fresh or in combination with some style of pastry. However, over the years Italian restaurants in America felt that they were not meeting the needs of their customers, so any number of creamy confections were concocted. Tiramisu is a good example. I think tiramisu is great if it's made right. I have, however, had to swallow so many poor interpretations of this rich dessert that I now think twice before ordering it.

Rich and creamy desserts—cassata, cheesecake, zuppa Inglese, bomboloni (custard-filled doughnuts), zabaglione—were not an everyday or every-week consideration in our house; those were desserts reserved for special holidays. More common were a simple rice pudding, a peach or strawberry crostata, or some type of biscotti and coffee.

It would have been easy to fill this chapter with desserts made with cream and custards and deliciously sinful cheese creations made with rich, rich mascarpone cheese. The challenge was to fashion tasty desserts *without* the fat and cholesterol. I think you will enjoy what I have created. I am particularly fond of the shortcake with strawberries, because it is loaded with flavor but has practically no fat. And I encourage you to try one of the biscotti recipes.

Pasta Frolla con Fragole

(Shortcake with Strawberries)

This shortcake is a snap to make, and the end result is a thick yet light and moist cake that works nicely not only with strawberries but with peaches and blueberries as well. The real plus is that my adaptation omits the eggs and butter from this classic pastry.

....

1 pint or more fresh
   strawberries, hulled and
   sliced thin
1 teaspoon kirsch
2 cups unbleached all-purpose
   flour
3 tablespoons sugar
2 teaspoons baking powder
1 teaspoon salt
1 tablespoon grated lemon
   zest
About 1¼ cups ricotta
   cheese, whipped with a
   spoon

1. Preheat the oven to 425°F. In a small bowl, toss the strawberries with the kirsch. Set aside, but do not refrigerate.

2. In a mixing bowl, combine the flour, sugar, baking powder, and salt. Stir well.

3. Add the lemon zest and the ricotta to the flour mixture. Stir vigorously to combine and form a ragged ball of dough. Turn the dough out onto a lightly floured surface and knead gently until the dough is soft yet not sticky, 6 to 8 minutes.

4. Place the dough on a lightly greased flat cookie sheet and press the dough into a circle about 7 inches in diameter.

5. Bake the cake for 30 to 35 minutes, until the top is lightly browned and the cake is cooked through. Place the cake on a wire rack to cool. (The cake can be made a day ahead or frozen for later use.)

6. Slice the cake in half horizontally. Spoon some of the juice from the strawberries onto the bottom half of the cake. Add the strawberries and place the top half of the cake over the strawberries. Press down gently on the top. Slice into wedges and serve with low-fat ice cream if desired.

Makes 1 7- to 8-inch cake, about 8 slices
Calories: 195 per 1-slice serving

DESSERTS

Pesche con Amaretti

(Peaches with Amaretti Cookies)

Sweet peaches and the slightly bitter flavor of almonds in the liqueur and cookies combine in this fruit crisp.

1. Preheat the broiler. In a medium-size bowl, toss together the peaches, lemon juice, and Amaretto. Set aside for 10 minutes, but do not refrigerate.

2. In a small bowl, combine the ground cookies (a food processor does the job nicely), brown sugar, and butter to form a coarse crumblike mixture.

3. Pack the peaches in one layer on a cookie sheet or an ovenproof pan and place the pan under the preheated broiler. Broil the peaches for 5 to 7 minutes, until tender. Leave the broiler on.

4. Sprinkle the cookie crumb mixture over the peaches and return the pan to the broiler. Broil for 1 to 2 minutes, until the topping is golden brown.

4 (about 2 pounds) ripe peaches, peeled, pitted, and cut into ¼-inch slices
1 tablespoon fresh lemon juice
1 teaspoon Amaretto liqueur (optional)
½ cup ground Amaretti cookies
2 teaspoons light brown sugar
1 tablespoon unsalted butter, cut into bits

Serves 4
Calories: 160 per serving

Pera e Ricotta

(Pears and Ricotta Cheese)

More often than not an Italian meal ends with cheese and fruit. Here, few ingredients produce a dessert having a mélange of flavors without depending on sugar or fat.

....

8 ounces low-fat ricotta cheese
2 tablespoons skim milk
1 lemon
2 quarts cold water
4 (about 2 pounds) very ripe
    Bartlett or Anjou pears
½ cup toasted slivered
    almonds (see Note)

1. In a medium-size bowl, beat the ricotta cheese with the milk until smooth. Refrigerate until ready to use.

2. Cut the lemon in half and squeeze the juice into the cold water; add the lemon halves to the water. Stem, peel, halve, and core the pears. Put them in the lemon water and refrigerate for up to 2 hours.

3. Drain the pears and put two halves on each of four dessert plates. Top each pear half with some of the cheese mixture. Sprinkle some of the toasted almonds over each plate.

Note: Preheat the oven to 375°F. Spread the almonds on a baking sheet and toast them for about 8 minutes.

Serves 4
Calories: 296 per serving

Biscotti con Nocciole

(Hazelnut Biscotti)

This crunchy Italian cookie is most often served as an accompaniment to espresso or coffee at the end of a meal.

....

1. Preheat the oven to 375°F. Spread the hazelnuts on a baking sheet and toast them for about 8 minutes. While still warm, rub the hazelnuts together in a kitchen towel to remove the brown skin. Close the ends of the towel and pound the nuts with a rolling pin. There should be some that are whole and some that are finely chopped.

2. In a medium-size bowl, cream the butter with the sugar. Beat in the eggs one at a time. Add the vanilla. Combine the flour, baking powder, and salt and add to the butter mixture. Fold in the nuts.

3. Preheat the oven to 350°F. Form the dough into two rolls, each about 8 inches long, flat across the top, rounded at the edges, and a bit less than ¾ inch high. Place the rolls on a lightly buttered baking sheet and bake for about 30 minutes or until golden brown. Remove the rolls from the oven and slice them about ¾ inch thick on the diagonal. Spread the slices on a wire rack set on a baking sheet and return the biscotti to the oven for another 10 minutes. Cool and store in airtight tins or jars.

¼ pound shelled hazelnuts
4 tablespoons unsalted butter
¼ cup sugar
2 large eggs
¼ teaspoon vanilla extract
1 cup unbleached all-purpose flour
1 teaspoon baking powder
¼ teaspoon salt

Makes 2 dozen biscotti
Calories: 59 per 1-biscotti serving

Mostaccioli di Ciccolata

(Chocolate and Walnut Biscotti)

Very often the conclusion of a meal in Italy is nothing more than biscotti dunked in a sweet dessert wine such as Vin Santo or moscato.

1 cup (about ¼ pound)
  walnut halves
2 ounces unsweetened
  chocolate
3 tablespoons unsalted butter
1¼ cups unbleached all-
  purpose flour
1 teaspoon baking powder
2 large eggs
½ cup sugar

1. Preheat the oven to 350°F. Put the walnuts on a cookie sheet and toast them for 8 minutes. Cool and chop coarse.

2. Melt the chocolate and butter in a double boiler over barely simmering water. Remove from the heat and beat until smooth. Let cool for 20 minutes.

3. Sift together the flour and baking powder. In a medium-size bowl, beat the eggs lightly. Add the sugar and blend well. Stir in the chocolate and blend well. Stir in the flour and baking powder mixture and combine well. Fold in the walnuts.

4. Preheat the oven to 350°F. On a lightly greased cookie sheet, form the dough into a roll about 14 inches long by 2 to 3 inches wide. Smooth the top and round the sides with a spatula.

5. Bake the biscotti for 35 to 40 minutes or until firm in the center. Remove the baking sheet from the oven and slice the biscotti on the diagonal into ½-inch-wide slices. Place the sliced biscotti on a wire rack set on the baking sheet and return the biscotti to the oven to bake for an additional 15 minutes. Cool and store in airtight tins or jars.

Makes about 2 dozen biscotti
Calories: 103 per 1-biscotti serving

DESSERTS

Espresso Granite

(Coffee Ice)

....

1. In a small bowl, combine the espresso, sugar, and Sambuca and refrigerate until well chilled.

2. Pour the mixture into ice cube trays or a shallow pan and place it in the freezer. Stir the mixture every 20 to 25 minutes for about 1 hour. Serve the granite in tall dessert or champagne glasses accompanied by Vin Santo wine.

2 cups freshly brewed espresso, chilled
3 tablespoons sugar
2 teaspoons Sambuca

Serves 4 to 6
Calories: 30 per serving

Granite di Limone

(Lemon Ice)

....

3 cups water
1 cup sugar
Minced zest of 1 lemon
½ cup fresh lemon juice

1. Put the water in a saucepan and add the sugar. Bring the liquid to a boil, lower the heat, and simmer, uncovered, for 5 minutes, stirring until the sugar has dissolved. Refrigerate until well chilled.

2. In a bowl, combine the sugar syrup, lemon zest, and lemon juice. Pour the granite into metal ice cube trays or a shallow metal pan and place in the freezer. Stir the granite every 30 minutes for about 1½ hours.

Makes about 1 quart
Calories: 100 per ½-cup serving

Ricotta al Espresso

(Whipped Ricotta with Espresso)

This is a dessert you can count on when guests show up unannounced. Creamy and rich-tasting with a mousselike consistency, it can be indulged in without guilt.

....

1. Put the ricotta cheese, sugar, coffee, and Sambuca in a food processor fitted with the steel blade and process until creamy and thick. Spoon the mixture into tall serving glasses and refrigerate for at least 2 hours, until thoroughly chilled.

2. Just before serving, sprinkle some of the chopped pistachios over the cheese.

Serves 4 to 6
Calories: 171 per serving

1 15-ounce carton low-fat ricotta cheese
½ cup confectioners' sugar
¼ cup freshly brewed espresso, cooled
2 tablespoons Sambuca or anisette
¼ cup finely chopped pistachios

Semifreddo al Lampone

A classic semifreddo is made with heavy cream, eggs, and egg whites and is put in the freezer overnight. I have eliminated the fat and the freezing, yet this dessert has the characteristics and flavor of the classic preparation.

....

1 15-ounce carton low-fat ricotta cheese
½ cup sugar
2 teaspoons kirsch or light rum
2 cups fresh raspberries or 1 10-ounce package frozen, thawed and drained through a fine-mesh sieve into a bowl
3 tablespoons sugar
Fresh strawberries or mint sprigs for garnish

1. Put the ricotta, sugar, and kirsch in a food processor fitted with the steel blade and process until creamy and smooth. Transfer the ricotta mixture to a 1- to 1½-quart serving bowl. Refrigerate.

2. In a food processor fitted with the steel blade, process the raspberries with the sugar to form a smooth puree.

3. Using a small knife, swirl the raspberry puree through the ricotta mixture and decoratively across the top. Cover and refrigerate for at least 4 hours. Spoon into individual dessert dishes. Garnish with fresh strawberries or fresh mint.

Serves 4
Calories: 301 per serving

INDEX